A2 Business Studies
UNIT 6

AQA

Module 6: External Influences and Objectives and Strategy

Gwen Coates

Series Editor: John Wolinski

Philip Allan Updates
Market Place
Deddington
Oxfordshire
OX15 0SE

tel: 01869 338652
fax: 01869 337590
e-mail: sales@philipallan.co.uk
www.philipallan.co.uk

© Philip Allan Updates 2002

ISBN-13: 978-0-86003-495-7
ISBN-10: 0-86003-495-X

This Guide has been written specifically to support students preparing for the AQA A2 Business Studies Unit 6 examination. The content has been neither approved nor endorsed by AQA and remains the sole responsibility of the author.

Printed by MPG Books, Bodmin

Environmental information
The paper on which this title is printed is sourced from managed, sustainable forests.

Contents

Introduction

■ ■ ■

Content Guidance

EXTERNAL INFLUENCES

Economic opportunities and constraints

Governmental opportunities and constraints

Social and other opportunities and constraints

OBJECTIVES AND STRATEGY

Impact on firms of a change in size

Business objectives

Business strategy

■ ■ ■

Questions and Answers

Introduction

About this guide

This Student Unit Guide has been written to support revision for AQA Unit 6, A2 business studies. After this introductory note on the aims and assessment of A-level, the guide is divided into two sections: Content Guidance and Questions and Answers.

The first section offers concise coverage of Module 6: External Influences and Objectives and Strategy. It combines an overview of key terms and concepts with an identification of opportunities to illustrate the higher-level skills of analysis and evaluation. The scope for linking different topic areas is also shown.

The second section provides six questions. The first five questions focus on a specific area of content in the same order as the first section. The sixth question is integrated, with a heavy weighting towards issues related to business strategy. Each question is based on the format of the Unit 6 paper and is followed by two sample answers (an A-grade and a lower-grade response) interspersed with examiner's comments.

You should read the relevant topic areas in the Content Guidance section before attempting a question from the Question and Answer section, and only read the specimen answers after you have tackled the questions.

Aims of the A-level qualification

A-level business studies aims to encourage candidates to:
- develop a critical understanding of organisations, the markets they serve and the process of adding value
- be aware that business behaviour can be studied from the perspectives of a range of stakeholders including customers, managers, creditors, owners/shareholders and employees
- acquire a range of skills including decision-making and problem-solving
- be aware of current business structure and practice

Assessment

A-level papers are designed to test certain skills. **Every mark that is awarded on an A-level paper is given for the demonstration of a skill.** The content of the course (the theories, concepts and ideas) provides a framework to allow students to show their skills. Recognising the content on its own is not enough to merit high marks. The following skills are tested:

- **Knowledge and understanding** — recognising and describing business concepts and ideas.
- **Application** — being able to explain or apply your understanding.
- **Analysis** — developing a line of thought in order to demonstrate its impact or consequences.
- **Evaluation** — making a judgement by weighing up the evidence provided.

Unit 6 assessment

Unit 6 tests the content of A2 Module 6, External Influences and Objectives and Strategy. The skill of evaluation has greater weighting than in Units 4 and 5 and forms 40% of the total marks. Consequently, the specification provides many opportunities for both analysis and evaluation, and examples of these are listed at the end of each of the book's Content Guidance topics. Bear this in mind during your preparations and revision, as you will need to practise evaluating and judging arguments.

Another important issue to note about Unit 6 is that it is a synoptic assessment in the form of a case study. A synoptic assessment is one that involves the integration of knowledge, understanding and skills learned in different parts of the A-level course. This means that it assesses your understanding of the relationship between the different aspects of business studies and requires you to use knowledge and skills acquired throughout the course. Several areas of the subject content may be assessed using integrating themes, which emphasise the interactive nature of the business world and draw the subject content together.

The Unit 6 case study paper is weighted so that marks are awarded as follows:

Unit 6 assessment objectives	Weighting
Knowledge: how well you know the meaning of theories, concepts and ideas	20%
Application: how well you use the information provided to explain benefits, problems, calculations and situations	15%
Analysis: how well you develop ideas, apply theory, consider implications and links between issues	25%
Evaluation: how well you judge the overall significance of the situation	40%

This compares with the figures for A2 overall, which are as follows:

Overall A2 assessment objectives	Weighting
Knowledge	20%
Application	20%
Analysis	26%
Evaluation	34%

The skills requirement of a question

A good guide to the skills requirement of a question is to look at the trigger or key words used in the questions. Specific trigger or key words will be used to indicate when you are being asked to analyse or evaluate. Because of the extent to which the skill of evaluation is tested in Unit 6, the trigger or key word in each question is likely to indicate evaluation. The A2 Unit 6 exam is likely to include some of the following words:

- 'Assess...'
- 'Comment upon...'
- 'Evaluate...'
- 'Consider...'
- 'To what extent...'
- 'Provide a reasoned judgement...'

In questions requiring evaluation, try to ensure that you provide a detailed conclusion and that you demonstrate judgement in weighing up the relative importance of different arguments. But remember that evaluation must be based on sound analysis. Students who fail to analyse generally do so because they have not developed their arguments. Analysis must be based on sound logic and/or the integration of business theory or concepts into an argument.

Although application has a lower weighting (15%) for Unit 6 than for other units, it is still an essential skill. The quality of a judgement invariably relies on the context of the question, and so your ability to apply your conclusion to the situation in the case study will help to earn both application and evaluation marks.

It is worth noting when studying for Unit 6 that questions involving the interpretation of numerical data and definition questions will be limited. Within the specification, the main areas that lend themselves to interpretation of data are economic opportunities and constraints (issues such as interest rates, exchange rates, inflation and unemployment) and decision trees (which requires an understanding of numerical areas such as probabilities and the construction and evaluation of decision tree diagrams). Most of the other sections do not contain reference to numerical data, thus limiting the scope for numerical questions on this examination paper. Using the sample questions in the guide for examination practice will enable you to recognise the impact this may have on your time management.

Revision strategies

Below is a list of general pieces of advice for examination preparation:
- Prepare well in advance.
- Organise your files, ensuring there are no gaps.
- Read about different approaches — there is no single right approach to business studies. Experience as many views and methods as possible. Read newspapers and business articles regularly throughout the A-level course.
- When reading an article, try to think of types of question an examiner might ask and how you would answer them. Your Unit 6 case study will be based on a business scenario and wide reading will help to familiarise you with a variety of businesses and circumstances.
- Take notes as you read. These will help to:
  - put the text into your own words, cementing your understanding
  - summarise and emphasise key points
  - focus your attention
  - précis information that could help with future revision
  - boost your morale by showing an end product of your revision sessions

- Develop and use your higher-level skills. Make sure that your revision is not dominated by factual knowledge alone. Check you can explain and analyse the points covered, and try to imagine situations in which evaluation can be applied.
- Practise examination questions. Use the questions in this book (and past papers when available) to improve your technique, making sure you complete all the questions in the time allowed. In the examination, you have 90 minutes to read the case study and answer the questions. Allowing 10 minutes for reading, you have 80 minutes to earn 80 marks, so allocate 1 minute to each mark available on the question. Thus if the question is worth 12 marks, you can devote 12 minutes to it.
- Maintain your motivation. Reward yourself for achieving targets, but do not get demoralised if you fall behind. If necessary, amend your objectives to a more realistic level.
- Find out the dates and times of your examinations and use this to prepare a detailed schedule for the study leave/examination period, making sure you build in time for relaxation and sleep.
- Focus on all the areas relevant to Unit 6 as questions covering all the topics comprising Modules 4 and 5 will be included. Do not merely focus on your favourite topics. Your revision is more likely to add value if it improves your understanding of an area you find difficult. Revising a topic you already know is a morale booster, but is it as valuable?
- Top up your memory just before the examination. If there are concepts, formulae or ratios that you find difficult, revisit them just before the examination.
- Adopt your own strategy. Everyone has a different learning style: use one that suits you.

Content
Guidance

This section of the guide outlines the topic areas of Module 6, which are as follows:
- economic opportunities and constraints
- governmental opportunities and constraints
- social and other opportunities and constraints
- impact on firms of a change in size
- business objectives
- business strategy

Read through the relevant topic areas before attempting to use the Question and Answer section.

Key concepts

Key concepts are all defined, but you should also have a business studies dictionary to hand.

Analysis

Under this heading there are suggestions on how topic areas could lend themselves to analysis. During your course and the revision period, you should refer to these opportunities. Test and practise your understanding of the variety of ways in which a logical argument or line of reasoning can be developed.

Evaluation

Opportunities for evaluation are highlighted under this heading within particular topic areas.

Links

This directs attention to other parts of the specification. The links are provided to encourage you to integrate your understanding of different topic areas.

Integration

The AQA specification states that external influences should be studied by looking at their effects on business decision-making and ability to meet objectives. It builds on all the AS and A2 subject content and particularly the external influences section of Module 3, which students should revisit before starting revision for this section. Objectives and strategy draws together all other modules and should be seen as integrating themes that emphasise the interactive nature of the business world. The section builds on the AS and A2 subject content and students should revisit the objectives and strategy material covered in AS Module 3.

EXTERNAL INFLUENCES

Economic opportunities and constraints

Before beginning revision on this area, ensure that you revisit and revise the content of AS Module 3 first. You need to be able to consider macroeconomic variables, including interest rates, exchange rates, inflation, unemployment and the business cycle, and how changes in these or the level of these influence business strategy.

Implications for business strategy of changes in macroeconomic variables

Interest rates

Interest rates are essentially the price of money, which is the cost of borrowing money and the reward for lending money. Interest rates in the UK are set by the Monetary Policy Committee of the Bank of England and not by the government. Changes in interest rates affect business in many different ways. For example, a fall in interest rates can have the following effects:

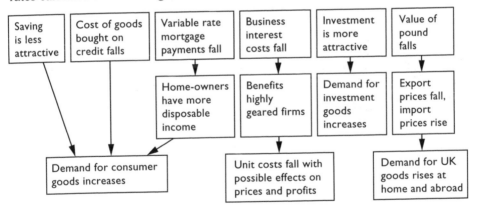

The resulting increase in demand may lead to an increase in output. More employees may be needed. Competition in the labour market might increase, leading to skill shortages and increasing wage costs. The increasing demand for goods and increasing wage demands may be inflationary.

Ensure that you can analyse the effects of a rise in interest rates — see the AS Unit 3 guide.

Exchange rates

The exchange rate is the price of one currency in terms of another. UK exchange rates are determined by supply and demand for the pound sterling.

Why demand pounds sterling?

Foreign individuals and organisations wishing to buy UK products or invest in the UK need pounds in order to do this. They exchange their own currency for pounds.

Why supply pounds?

British individuals and organisations wishing to buy foreign products or invest abroad need foreign currency in order to do this. They exchange pounds for other currency.

The value of sterling

High UK interest rates will encourage more investment in the UK, hence increasing the demand for pounds and thus the exchange rate of the pound. A strong pound is likely to lead to an increase in export prices and a fall in import prices, thus reducing the competitiveness of UK industry both at home and abroad.

Will export prices rise?

This depends on whether businesses are prepared to absorb the rise in the exchange rate and reduce their profit margins. If they do this, they could leave prices unchanged.

Are rising export prices always a bad thing?

The effect on sales and sales revenue will depend on the price elasticity of demand for the exports. For inelastic goods, a rise in price will not really affect sales and may increase sales revenue. For elastic goods, a rise in price will reduce sales and sales revenue significantly.

Are falling import prices always a bad thing?

This depends on whether imported products are inputs for UK businesses or substitutes for UK products. Cheaper imported raw materials will mean UK production costs fall and hence prices of finished goods might be reduced. Cheaper imported substitutes will adversely affect UK sales, unless UK goods have a competitive advantage or a unique selling point.

Check that you can analyse the effects of falling exchange rates.

Constantly fluctuating exchange rates seriously affect business strategy because they:
- create uncertainty
- affect the ability to plan ahead effectively
- affect the ability or desire to exploit foreign markets
- may require the use of spot/future pricing in contracts, which can be costly
- may incur costs, if constantly updating pricing literature for overseas markets

Inflation

Inflation means a persistent rise in the average level of prices and is measured by the retail price index (RPI). In 1997, the UK government gave the Bank of England and its Monetary Policy Committee the responsibility of controlling inflation by the use of interest rate changes. It was given the specific target of keeping inflation at or below 2.5%. In January 2001, the inflation rate was 1.8%, the lowest recorded in 25 years.

A low level of inflation, as experienced in the UK at present, can have a number of effects on business strategy:
- low interest rates
- firms become more internationally competitive in relation to export markets and against imports
- less uncertainty in the economy means business is able to plan ahead, since prices (of goods for sale and of supplies) can be predicted more easily
- there are lower costs due to fewer price adjustments to, for example, price lists
- more certainty about short-term pricing decisions means more time for long-term strategic decision-making
- constantly rising prices mean poorly performing firms can record increasing sales and profits in nominal terms, but low inflation means such firms can't disguise poor sales performance or easily raise prices to cover their own inefficiency

Ensure that you understand the implications of increasing rates of inflation. Refer to the AS Unit 3 guide.

Unemployment

In June 2001, unemployment in the UK went below 1 million for the first time since 1975. Low levels of unemployment affect business strategy in two main ways:
- More people in work means more income and therefore more spending and increasing sales of normal or luxury goods.
- However, a tightening labour market makes it harder to recruit suitably skilled or qualified individuals. In such a situation, workers have more bargaining power and wage costs may therefore rise.

Ensure that you understand the implications of high levels of unemployment. Refer to the AS Unit 3 guide.

The business cycle

The business cycle is a regular pattern of rising and falling demand and output in an economy over a period of time. It is characterised by four main phases: boom, recession, slump and recovery. Depending on the nature of the products sold, some firms may be more affected by these phases than others. For example, construction firms are significantly affected by the business cycle but toothpaste manufacturers are unlikely to be affected. In addition, each phase of the cycle has different effects on business. A recession characterised by falling incomes and demand will affect firms selling normal or luxury products differently to those selling inferior products.

See the AS Unit 3 guide for a detailed consideration of the implications of each phase of the business cycle.

NB Normal or luxury goods are those for which demand increases as incomes rise and vice versa, e.g. fillet steak and other high-quality meat products. Inferior goods are those for which demand falls as incomes rise and vice versa, e.g. Spam and other inferior meat products.

Analysis Opportunities for analysis of these macroeconomic variables include:

- considering price elasticity of demand when examining the effects of a strong/weak pound on exports and imports
- considering income elasticity of demand when examining the effects of a rise/fall in income resulting from high/low levels of unemployment, and from different phases of the business cycle
- analysing the impact of different phases of the business cycle on business in general and on particular businesses
- considering the impact of high/low unemployment on different aspects of a business (sales, labour supply, costs etc.)
- studying the implications of high/low interest rates on different organisations or different aspects of an organisation (sales, investment, gearing etc.)
- examining the effects of inflation on business
- examining the impact of different macroeconomic variables on trading conditions for business in general or for particular businesses
- considering business strategy in relation to trading conditions in the economy
- analysing the impact of different economic variables on the labour market with respect to the creation of skills surpluses and skills shortages

Evaluation Opportunities for evaluation include:

- judging the relative impact of different macroeconomic variables on a business's short-term and long-term strategy
- considering the extent to which fluctuating exchange rates might affect a decision to enter new export markets
- assessing the extent to which a particular industry is affected by different phases of the business cycle or by any other macroeconomic variable
- judging the impact on the labour market of different economic changes, and their consequences for specific businesses

Links The effects of macroeconomic variables on business strategy link to activities such as pricing, budgeting, profitability, break-even, investment appraisal, labour recruitment and remuneration.

The labour market: skills surpluses and shortages

Causes of surpluses or shortages
- changes in education and training
- market changes
- wage levels

Impact of a skills surplus
- lowers workers' morale
- weakens the bargaining power of the workforce
- breaks up teams

Company reactions to a skills surplus
- retraining and multi-skilling

- redundancy
- lowering wages

Impact of a skills shortage
- strengthens the bargaining power of the workforce
- increases labour costs
- reduces international competitiveness

Company reactions to a skills shortage
- retraining and multi-skilling
- overseas recruitment
- poaching of workers
- outsourcing (contracting out)

Analysis Opportunities for analysis include:
- explaining the causes of a shortage (or surplus)
- examining the impact of the situation on a business
- considering the possible reactions of a business

Evaluation Opportunities for evaluation include:
- assessing the best strategies to avoid the problems or to take advantage of the situation
- evaluating the different impact on different businesses
- looking at the extent to which the firm could anticipate the shortages or surpluses

Links Possible links to other areas include the impact on methods of production (labour or capital intensive), the impact on recruitment and labour retention, and the relation to location decisions.

International competitiveness

Overview

International competition may be based on price competition and/or non-price competition. The more competitive a firm is in relation to its international rivals, the larger will be its global market share.

Internal factors

To be internationally competitive involves considering internal aspects such as production, marketing and human resource management. This might involve deciding how efficiency and productivity can be increased by:
- becoming more capital intensive and shedding labour
- introducing new technology
- introducing organisational strategies

Overseas competitiveness could also involve increasing marketing efforts and considering how new areas of demand can be created. In this context, international competitiveness might be improved by benchmarking, where individual companies become aware of the need to compete with the best in the world.

External factors

A firm must also consider external factors, such as relative inflation rates, business cycles in different countries, the degree of trade protection (e.g. import controls) and the strength of exchange rates.

Revisit the previous section to confirm your understanding of these external factors.

Any or all of these factors will determine the extent to which firms are internationally competitive. For example, low inflation in the UK will benefit exporters since, in relative terms, UK goods will be more price competitive. However, if the pound is strong, export prices might have to be increased, thus cancelling out the benefits of low inflation.

Whether export prices are increased following a rise in the exchange rate of the pound depends on the price elasticity of demand for the product. It also depends on whether the firm can accept a lower profit margin, which will, in turn, depend upon the financial state of the business. At the same time, imports will be cheaper and thus firms will face pressures to maintain and improve their efficiency.

This analysis is further complicated for firms that export goods abroad but use imports as inputs. In such a situation all angles need to be considered.

Analysis Opportunities for analysis of international competitiveness include:
- examining the exchange rate risk involved in the decision to enter export markets
- considering the amount of trade done with different countries and the effect of exchange rate changes of any one currency
- the implications of membership (or non-membership) of the euro on business
- analysing the determinants of international competitiveness for a particular firm in terms of production, people, marketing and strategic issues

Evaluation Opportunities for evaluation include:
- judging the importance of uncertainty and risks when trading abroad and the need to balance this with the desire to expand markets
- assessing the extent to which international markets are more competitive than domestic markets
- assessing the extent to which non-membership of the euro will influence the competitiveness of UK firms in Europe
- judging the relative importance of different determinants of international competitiveness in a particular situation

Links Possible links to other areas include operations management in relation to benchmarking and productivity, marketing in relation to pricing and non-price methods of promotion, people issues in relation to organisational structures and strategies, and business strategy and objectives in relation to whether and how businesses aim to become more competitive.

Economic growth

Definition of economic growth

Economic growth occurs when the level of economic activity increases. Essentially, it is the extent to which real (taking into account inflation) national income per head increases over time. The value of a country's economic activity is known as its gross national product (GNP) and can be measured in three ways: the income, output and expenditure methods.

The income method
Adding up all the income earned (rent, wages, salaries, interest and profit).

The output method
Adding up the value of all goods and services produced.

The expenditure method
Adding up consumer, business and government spending plus the balance of export less import spending.

Gross domestic product (GDP) is also used to measure economic growth. Like GNP, it measures the economic activity of a country, but it excludes net property income from abroad.

Determinants of economic growth

- A more efficient use of factors of production to provide more goods and services.
- Developing a competitive advantage in certain sectors of the economy in order to compete internationally, e.g. technology in the Far East.
- Exploitation of natural resources, e.g. oil in the Middle East and the North Sea.
- An increasing and more highly skilled labour force and a growing population.
- Increasing investment and technology.
- Government policy to encourage economic growth.

Effects of economic growth on business and the environment

- Favourable trading conditions and new business opportunities.
- More security and certainty, and therefore more confidence in planning for the future.
- Rising incomes, which lead to increased demand and sales revenue (but this depends on the income elasticity of demand for products).
- Market opportunities for existing products in existing and in new markets.
- Market opportunities for new, risky, products as a result of high levels of spending.

Economic growth and increased wealth do not necessarily produce an increase in welfare. Growth:

- can lead to negative externalities, e.g. increasing levels of pollution and congestion
- can harm the environment
- may be impossible to sustain in the long term as the world's resources run out
- is often accompanied by increasing costs of land, property and labour
- does not benefit firms selling inferior products or those with a low income elasticity of demand for their products
- may test a firm's ability to cope with a growing business in terms of organisational structures, personnel, technology, production capacity and finance

It is important to recognise that the level of economic activity and growth differs not only between countries but also within a particular country, with consequent effects on firms' international, national and regional markets.

Analysis Opportunities for analysis of economic growth include:

- examining the effect of economic growth on firms in different markets and with differing income elasticities of demand
- considering the disadvantages of economic growth and how these affect a firm's operations
- studying the determinants of economic growth

Evaluation Opportunities for evaluation include:

- judging the extent to which economic growth benefits firms in different markets
- assessing the impact of negative externalities resulting from economic growth on the operations and profitability of firms
- assessing the extent to which differences in wealth and the rate of economic growth between different regions of the UK might affect a firm with plants throughout the UK

Links Economic growth links to marketing issues such as marketing opportunities, competitive advantage and income elasticity of demand. There are also issues from operations management such as productivity, technology and investment. Finally, there are people issues including remuneration and recruitment.

The EU and other overseas opportunities in emerging markets

The European Union

The EU was formed on 1 November 1993 with the objective of removing trade barriers between member states and eventually forming a political and economic union. It consists of 15 member nations.

EU business advantages

- There is access to a market of 375 million people, which is bigger than Japan and the USA put together.
- The enlarged market allows increased specialisation to take place.
- The large market also provides opportunities for economies of scale and lower costs.
- More competition may lead to improved efficiency and therefore lower costs.
- More intense competition may encourage innovation.
- There are opportunities for more European mergers and joint ventures resulting in synergy and improved efficiency.
- There is encouragement for inward investment (e.g. by Japanese firms), which increases employment and income and opportunities for supplier industries.
- There is greater mobility of labour, giving firms a wider labour force to draw on.
- With firms more able to invest anywhere in the EU, there is greater mobility of capital.

EU business problems

- There is an increase in legislation and the need to meet common technical standards.
- There is increased competition both in Europe and in the domestic market.
- Labour and capital may be attracted to other European countries.

The euro

The euro is the single European currency that was introduced on 1 January 1999 and adopted by 11 EU countries. This group of countries, often known as the euro zone, comprises 80% of the EU population. The currencies of countries in the euro zone were fixed permanently to each other. Euro notes and coins were introduced on 1 January 2002, and by the end of June 2002, individual currencies will no longer be legal tender. The UK has not joined.

Advantages to businesses in the euro-zone

- No exchange rate transaction costs when trading within the euro zone.
- No need to use forward or spot markets when agreeing contracts in the euro zone.
- Price transparency makes it easier to compare prices within the euro zone.
- No uncertainty due to exchange rate changes. This encourages trade and makes financial forecasting more accurate.

There are, of course, disadvantages such as the transition costs of new electronic tills, computer software and staff training. In relation to these advantages and problems, it is important to consider the UK's decision not to adopt the euro in terms of:

- the effects on trade between UK businesses and firms within the euro zone
- the effects on business decisions about locating in the UK or in the euro zone
- the effects on price competitiveness

Opportunities in emerging markets

An emerging market is an international area that has the potential to grow and develop in terms of productive capacity, market opportunities and competitive advantage. Eastern Europe is a good example, where the fall of the communist regimes in the late 1980s has had the following implications for business in Europe:

- Eastern Europe's population of over 100 million is a major new market.
- There are market opportunities for new products and well-established branded products.
- Eastern European production costs are lower, with cheaper labour and land rents plus less stringent controls.
- The introduction of capitalism and the market system means new competition.

The transition from an emerging market to a fully developed market does not take place overnight and this results in a variety of problems including:

- Relatively low incomes.
- Unstable political regimes leading to unpredictable decision-making and sudden changes to trading conditions.
- High inflation, which affects confidence, and may lead to transactions being made in other currencies with relatively stable values, or even trade using barter.
- Problems raising finance in countries where the banking system needs developing or where there is no stock market.
- Relatively poor infrastructure, transport and communication systems.
- Markets for buying and selling may not be well developed.
- The experience of management and employees may be lacking in relation to a market- or profit-based approach to work and business.

Analysis Opportunities for analysis of overseas opportunities include:

- ensuring that responses are integrated in relation to the various functional areas within a business and the external environment
- examining the type of firm, its size and the type of market in which it operates
- considering the firm's objectives, trading position and resources, and the abilities of its management
- considering the possible effects of a single European currency on business

Evaluation Opportunities for evaluation include:

- discussing the extent to which a common marketing strategy will be adopted or separate ones for each market
- assessing the importance of balance between home markets and new overseas markets (or the difficulties of coordinating activities)
- judging the risks involved in overseas marketing opportunities against the benefits
- judging the impact of a single European currency, of which the UK is not a member, on UK business

Links Possible links to other areas include marketing strategies, economies of scale and efficiency issues, location of industry, impact of exchange rates on pricing and competitiveness, and EU legislation.

Governmental opportunities and constraints

Government policies affecting business

Economic policy

Governments have a range of macroeconomic policies available to them.

It is important to understand what these policies are and broadly how they work, and it is vital that you understand how they affect business.

Fiscal policy

Fiscal policy involves the use of taxation and government expenditure to influence the economy. It is often known as budgetary policy and is the responsibility of the chancellor of the exchequer. Initial changes in fiscal policy can have further multiplier effects on business and the economy.

Taxation
Taxation is a withdrawal of money from the economy in that it tends to reduce total spending and demand.

Government expenditure
Government expenditure is an injection of money into the economy and thus tends to increase total spending and demand.

A budget surplus
There is a budget surplus when taxation is greater than government spending. Overall spending and demand in the economy are reduced, leading to a fall in economic activity.

A budget deficit
There is a budget deficit when government spending is greater than taxation. It means overall spending and demand increase, leading to a rise in economic activity.

A balanced budget
This is when taxation is equal to government spending. Overall spending and demand in the economy remain unchanged, although specific industries and areas may see changes in economic activity.

Monetary policy

Monetary policy involves controlling the money supply and the rate of interest in order to influence the level of spending and demand in the economy. The current economic policy emphasis is on controlling interest rates rather than the money supply targets of the past.

Recap the previous section on interest rates.

If interest rates are too low, total demand in the economy may be greater than supply, leading to an increase in the rate of inflation. If interest rates are too high, total demand in the economy may be too low, leading to unemployment and problems for business. Initial changes in monetary policy can have further multiplier effects on business and the economy.

Intervention versus laissez-faire

Interventionist government policy is based on the belief that government should exert a strong influence on the economy, rather than allowing market forces to dictate conditions.

Examples of intervention include:
- counter-cyclical policies to alleviate the effects of the business cycle
- support for new firms and rescue packages for large manufacturing industries
- regional policy
- fixed exchange rates
- legislation to provide strong protection for consumers and workers
- wages councils
- competition policy

Laissez-faire government policy is based on the belief that the free market will maximise business efficiency and consumer satisfaction. It therefore tries to avoid interfering in the running of business or any other part of the economy.

Privatisation

This is when state-run industries are returned to the private sector. Examples include:
- contracting out of refuse services from local authorities
- deregulation of bus routes
- the transfer of nationalised industries into public limited companies
- the sale of government-owned assets

Arguments for privatisation
- There is a broadening of share ownership.
- The introduction of competition improves efficiency.
- Competition provides the consumer with more choice.

Arguments against privatisation
- Companies may exploit consumers in the provision of certain basic products, e.g. water, gas, electricity.
- Many nationalised industries were natural monopolies, meaning the most efficient means of production was via a single producer/supplier.

Watchdogs
The government has established regulatory bodies (watchdogs) such as OFGAS and

OFWAT to prevent privatised monopolies exploiting their markets. They have responsibility for:

- monitoring behaviour and pricing
- setting performance standards
- allowing new entrants to the industry

Analysis Opportunities for analysis of the way government policies affect
business include:

- recognising how the impact of policy will differ depending on the nature of the
  business and its products
- examining how privatisation of nationalised industries has opened them up to
  market forces and made them more efficient
- considering how regulation prevents private monopolies emerging
- assessing the implications of time lags in relation to economic policies and their
  effect on the economy and on business

Evaluation Opportunities for evaluation include:

- evaluating the extent to which regulation or deregulation promote efficiency
- assessing the extent to which firms are influenced by different government policies
- considering the overall desirability of government intervention in a situation

Links Possible links of government policy to other areas include macroeconomic
variables, particularly interest rates, and legislation and its influence on business.

Social and other opportunities and constraints

Social responsibilities

Definition of social responsibilities

*Check that you understand and recognise a firm's responsibility to employees, customers
and other stakeholders covered in the section on social responsibilities in the AS Unit 3
guide.*

Social responsibilities are the duties towards stakeholder groups, which a firm may
or may not accept. Accepting these duties makes good business sense because
integrating them into a firm's marketing strategy and objectives is likely to increase
the number of customers and save money. In addition, customer loyalty and workforce
morale are important factors in a firm's success, and meeting its social responsibilities in relation to these and other groups may promote this.

Accepting or ignoring the responsibilities

If social responsibilities are ignored, firms leave themselves open to pressure group action and also may not attract the employees, customers and investors they require. However, a firm cannot meet the needs of every stakeholder group and must decide priorities, which will depend on current conditions, the time scale involved and the nature of the firm. Where survival is threatened, a firm might have to opt for short-term profit rather than meeting its social responsibilities.

Business ethics

Definition of business ethics

This refers to codes of behaviour that are considered morally correct. These moral codes of behaviour or principles influence decision-making. Examples of ethical dilemmas are:

- Should an advertising agency accept work from a cigarette manufacturer?
- Should a bank invest in companies or countries that produce chemical weapons?
- Should a weapons manufacturer sell arms to a country that is politically unstable?
- Should a manufacturer of cosmetics test its products on animals?
- Should a firm reject the most profitable solution to a problem in favour of the one providing the greatest benefit to society?

Is ethical decision-making profitable?

Ethical decision-making can have marketing advantages, acting as a unique selling point (USP) or competitive advantage, but it might reduce profitability or conflict with existing policies. The positive effects of ethical decision-making depend very much on whether consumers are well informed and concerned. In some cases ethical policies may create a niche market.

Are all ethical decisions based on sound moral principles?

Public opinion and media pressure may force a firm to change its approach and adopt an ethical position. This is not really making an ethical decision, but simply responding to pressure after considering costs and benefits.

Delegation and ethics

There are two major influences on the moral behaviour of businesses:

(1) Organisations consist of individuals who have their own moral codes, values and principles.
(2) Firms have their own cultures and codes of behaviour that affect attitudes, decision-making and management style.

This distinction is important, especially when considering delegation and ethics.

Overall, it depends on which of these two influences is dominant, the corporate or the individual culture. If there is a conflict between the ethical position of the firm and the moral values of the individual, then delegated decision-making may not reflect the ethical stance of the firm. Firms should therefore invest in training and communication to ensure that all staff behave in an agreed ethical manner and that delegated activity is performed on an agreed ethical basis.

Environmental pressures and opportunities

External costs

Major environmental concerns include pollution, global warming, sustainable development and recycling. The environmental effects of a firm's activities are known as externalities and may be positive or negative. Social or external costs are the negative consequences of activities that are not paid for by the firm responsible, but by the public, other organisations, or the government. Because these social costs do not directly affect the profits of the firm generating them, there is no direct incentive for the firm to minimise them. This is a form of market failure and government intervention is often necessary to influence behaviour. Such intervention may take the form of:

- taxation to make the polluter pay
- legislation to ban or control certain activities
- licences that allow a certain level of activity to be undertaken

Cost–benefit analysis is an approach that weighs up the financial and social costs and benefits of any investment projects.

Environmental reputation

Many large companies have environmental policies aimed at minimising any damage their activities might have on the environment. Such policies include the contingency or disaster planning designed to limit the immediate impacts of a major environmental disaster and its long-term consequences for the company in terms of reputation and demand. A good environmental reputation can provide:

- marketing opportunities in terms of attracting customers, establishing brand loyalty and allowing premium pricing
- financial advantages in terms of ease of obtaining finance for investment
- human resource opportunities such as better applicants and a more motivated workforce

A bad reputation in this area can have adverse effects on customer perceptions of a firm and its products, on its ability to raise finance and on the attitude and quality of employees.

Environmental audits

Environmental audits are increasingly being used. These are independent checks on a firm's polluting activities, such as emissions, wastage levels and recycling.

Political change

Opportunities and constraints

Political change can create new opportunities or introduce new constraints. Examples include:

- The return of a Conservative government in 1979, which altered business conditions with a new emphasis on the importance of the market. The Conservatives introduced privatisation and deregulation and reduced considerably the power of trade unions.
- The political changes in eastern Europe in the late 1980s and 1990s, where market economies were introduced to replace the planned systems of the past.

See pages 20 and 22 for more detail on eastern Europe and privatisation.

Pressure group activity

The range of pressure groups

Pressure groups are organisations formed by people with a common interest or shared goal who get together in order to further their interests. They include single-issue pressure groups and those with ongoing concerns. Examples include:

- environmental groups such as Greenpeace
- employee groups such as trade unions
- consumer groups such as the Consumers' Association
- employer groups such as the CBI (Confederation of British Industry)
- animal rights groups such as the World Wildlife Fund
- human rights groups such as Amnesty International

Pressure group activity usually aims to change:

- the actions of business
- public opinion using the media and public relations

Pressure groups are stakeholders. If they can convince business they are valid stakeholders and therefore represent the views of people affected by business actions, they are more likely to be taken seriously. If they are not considered to be valid stakeholders, they will be ignored or their arguments disputed and discredited. The success of a pressure group is determined by:

- the financial resources available for public relations (PR) activities
- its reputation and the strength of its argument

- public sympathy for its cause
- access to politicians and the media
- the quality of response from the business

Firms' responses to pressure group activity include:
- agreement and change
- launching a PR campaign to counter and discredit the pressure group's claims
- lobbying parliament via trade associations

Lobbying involves putting a viewpoint across directly to government ministers and MPs, who can vote on particular pieces of legislation or encourage new laws.

Whether a business should agree with pressure group demands depends on how powerful the pressure group is and how its demands might affect the business.

An important point to remember when answering any question on this issue is to keep focused on the way in which pressure group activity affects business.

Social auditing

Purpose

This is the process by which a business attempts to assess the impact of the entire range of its activities on stakeholders and society in general. It is part of the move towards more scrutiny of business practices and increased availability of information for consumers and pressure groups.

It often results in the production of a set of social accounts and attempts to evaluate performance against a set of non-financial criteria, e.g. effects on the environment and attempts to meet social obligations to employees. Instead of financial ratios such as profit margins and return on capital (ROC), social ratios are used to specify such variables as average life of products, the percentage of recycled materials used and industrial accidents per 100 workers.

Implementation

A social audit is likely to include details about:
- pollution
- waste
- workforce health and safety
- details of salary differences between the highest and lowest paid employees
- the extent to which employees are valued
- views of consumers about whether the business is living up to its ideals

Social auditing involves:
- identifying social objectives and ethical values
- defining stakeholders

- establishing social performance indicators
- measuring performance, keeping records and preparing social accounts
- submitting accounts to independent audit and publishing the results

Benefits

A social audit is beneficial in:

- providing information to pressure groups and consumers about the social responsibility of business
- identifying the extent to which a firm is meeting its non-financial objectives
- giving employees a picture of the impact of a firm's activities
- deterring future criticism, especially if the social audit is independently scrutinised

As in the previous section on environmental pressures and opportunities, the social or external costs of a firm's activities constitute a form of market failure that may lead to government intervention.

Analysis Opportunities for analysis include:

- comparing the factors that lead to successful pressure group activity
- studying the pros and cons of a firm accepting its social responsibilities
- examining the influence on business ethics of a firm's decision-making processes
- considering the pressures and opportunities that arise from environmental issues

Evaluation Opportunities for evaluation include:

- assessing whether a firm should accept its social responsibilities
- discussing the potential conflict that could occur between business ethics and individual moral principles when decision-making is delegated
- judging the extent to which a firm should and is able to take responsibility for environmental issues
- evaluating the impact of pressure group activity on a firm's decision-making activity

Links Possible links to other areas include people and delegation, and common and conflicting objectives of stakeholders.

OBJECTIVES AND STRATEGY

Objectives and Strategy at A2 draws together the entire subject content of other areas and must be considered as integrating themes. You should therefore revisit all other areas of the specification, especially AS Module 3 (see AS Unit 3 guide).

Impact on firms of a change in size

Introduction

Reasons for the growth of firms might include:
- opportunities to take advantage of economies of scale
- greater likelihood of remaining competitive
- growth by diversification allowing for the spreading of risk
- a large company with plenty of assets finds it easier to ride out recession and other changes in the economy
- opportunities for extra profit
- possible benefits to stakeholders

Financing growth

It is important to focus on the issues of sufficient and relevant forms of finance for both start-up and/or growing firms rather than simply listing and briefly explaining all sources of finance. Revise your knowledge of the sources of finance from AS Module 1, but focus on their application to start-up/growth.

In addition, remember that:
- *steady growth is preferable to rapid growth because it minimises risks and spreads the need for funding, making finance easier to obtain*
- *growth is a long-term strategy needing long-term finance*
- *growth is not always the best strategy, in that sometimes a company will need to refocus on its core business and get rid of costly areas from earlier growth phases*

Sources of finance

Internal sources	External sources	
	Short term	Long term
Retained profit	Trade credit	Share capital
Controlling working capital	Debt factoring	Bank loan
Sale and lease-back of assets	Bank overdraft	Debentures
Asset sales	Hire purchase	Venture capital
	Leasing	Grants

The most appropriate source of finance will depend upon:

- the type of business — whether a sole trader, partnership or limited company
- the stage of business development — whether a new or an established business
- the circumstances and performance of the business — whether it has a good track record, whether it has collateral
- the state of the economy — whether boom or recession
- the attitude of shareholders — whether they want an immediate return on investment or are happy to forgo short-term dividends so that profit can be retained and used
- the actual cost of finance — interest rates for loans, advertising and administrative costs for share issues
- the level of gearing and the risks involved if interest rates change
- the use of funds — whether for fixed assets or for working capital needs
- the timing: short term being 1 year, medium term being 1–5 years and long term being over 5 years

Over-trading

An important issue to consider in relation to financing growth is when a business fails to obtain appropriate finance. This places a strain on working capital and can force a firm into liquidation. It is therefore vital to arrange finance in advance in order to ensure there are sufficient funds to meet short-term financial commitments.

Cash flow planning

Cash flow planning is the second growth issue and is as important for a growing business as it is for a start-up; there are new assets to buy and working capital is needed for extra raw materials and labour costs.

Ensure that you revise the difference between cash and profit, and the effects of financing growth on the balance sheet and the financial ratios, especially the gearing ratio. In relation to this, revise material from Module 4 on ratio analysis.

Analysis Opportunities for analysis of a change in business size include:

- examining the factors that lead to over-trading and the consequences of over-trading for business
- assessing the differences between cash and profit and the importance of cash flow planning in facilitating growth
- considering the factors that determine the most appropriate source of finance for a growing business

Evaluation Opportunities for evaluation include:

- selecting and justifying a source of finance to fund the growth of a business
- evaluating the extent to which effective management of finance is the key to successful growth

Links Possible links to other areas include accounting and finance areas such as sources of finance, the distinction between cash flow and profit, cash flow management and ratio analysis.

Management reorganisation during growth

Recognise that growth is difficult to manage, especially if it is rapid. Successful growth requires strong and effective management.

Problems of adjustment

The following are issues to consider when a business grows and the owner/boss becomes the owner/manager:

- Management structures and hierarchies change, often from simple functional structures to complex matrix or regional structures.
- New layers of authority and new departments are created, meaning that the management process becomes more complex.
- There is more delegation and therefore a loss of direct contact with customers and staff; the manager takes on more of a coordinating role.
- Staff and staff responsibilities will need to be changed.
- Changes resulting from growth may be difficult to achieve and may have adverse effects on staff in terms of motivation and team spirit, and consequent effects on customers.
- Managing and motivating a large team successfully is likely to require less autocratic leadership and management styles.

Loss of direction and control

Major problems that might result from growth include a loss of focus or direction and a loss of control due to poor management of staff. These are human resource issues caused by greater demands placed on a senior management that must manage and motivate a larger team.

Analysis Opportunities for analysis of business reorganisation include:
- considering the reluctance of owner/managers to delegate as a business grows and examining the problems that this might cause
- examining the difference between the role of owner/boss and owner/manager as a business grows

Evaluation Opportunities for evaluation include:
- assessing the problems involved in managing a growing business
- judging whether an entrepreneur's managerial style should change as their business grows

Links Possible links to other areas are people in organisations, including management structures, delegation, motivation and leadership, plus communication in large organisations.

Problems of transition in size

From private to publicly quoted

Problems often arise when growth involves changing from private to public limited company status. However, a number of companies have changed back from plc to private limited company status (Virgin and the Body Shop, for example) because this allows more privacy and less pressure on management resulting from share price movements. This, in turn, allows management to take a longer-term view.

Ensure that you revise the meaning, characteristics and implications of different forms of ownership as covered in AS Module 3/AS Unit 3 guide.

From national to international

Growth involving a change from a national to an international operation is often a difficult process. Issues to consider include local markets, consumer tastes and attitudes, location of sales outlets, and control and delegation of authority to local management. Organisations such as Sock Shop, Laura Ashley, and Marks and Spencer have not been particularly successful in moving abroad; what works in the UK doesn't necessarily work elsewhere.

Retrenchment

Just as problems arise from the growth of firms, they also arise as a result of firms cutting back the scale of their operations. Different types of retrenchment affect organisations and stakeholder groups in different ways.

Stop recruiting/offer early retirement/voluntary redundancy
The effects are that:
- job insecurity might be reduced
- excellent or key staff may leave
- there are fewer opportunities to introduce change and structure the business

Rationalisation by delayering
The effects are that:
- there is less impact on production and operations at shop-floor level
- it might empower or enrich remaining jobs
- there is an increased workload for remaining management and possibly increased stress
- there is a loss of promotion prospects as a layer of opportunity disappears

Rationalisation by closing a section of the business

The effects are that:

- it reduces fixed costs and therefore break-even quantity
- capacity utilisation may rise in other sections of the business
- there is no going back once a factory is closed even if the economy booms
- there may be the loss of many good staff with valuable skills

Making targeted cutbacks and redundancies throughout the business

The effects are that:

- it should allow the business to re-organise to meet its objectives
- it could get rid of less productive staff, thus improving overall performance
- there may be a feeling of job insecurity and lack of trust among remaining staff

Analysis Opportunities for analysis of reorganisation during growth include:

- examining the problems that may occur for a growing firm that changes from private limited (ltd) to public limited (plc) status
- considering why a firm might change back from plc to private limited status
- assessing the effect of different types of retrenchment on a business and on its stakeholders

Evaluation Opportunities for evaluation include:

- assessing the extent to which successful UK firms can duplicate their success by operating in international markets
- evaluating the type of retrenchment that is likely to have the least adverse effects on the workforce or on particular stakeholder groups

Links Problems of transition in size link to accounting and finance in relation to cash flow management, people in relation to motivation and management structures, and operations management in relation to operational efficiency.

Change in ownership

Types of growth

Growth can be achieved either internally/organically or externally.

Internal/organic

This type of expansion is from within the firm rather than via integration with another firm; finance is usually from retained profit in a process of growth that is slow but less risky.

External growth

This type of expansion is via the integration of two or more companies by takeover or merger; this process of growth is much quicker than organic growth but, given the problems of integrating two separate organisations, can be risky. A merger is where two or more firms agree to come together under one board of directors. A takeover is where one firm buys a majority shareholding in another firm and therefore assumes full management control. Takeovers can be hostile or friendly.

Forms of integration

In general, integration may result in the benefits of synergy (1 + 1 = 3), which means the resulting organisation is more efficient and powerful than the two organisations separately. A major problem in almost every case is resistance to change, especially coping with workforce fears about jobs changing or disappearing.

Vertical

This describes integration between firms operating at the preceding or succeeding stages of the production process. Integrating backward is when a manufacturing business integrates with suppliers of raw materials, and integrating forward is with retailers of the finished product. Its benefits are:
- control over supplies in terms of price, quality and reliability
- control over the sale of products to the final consumer, marketing image etc.
- absorption of profit margins of integrated supplier/retailer

Horizontal

This describes integration between firms operating at the same stage of production and in the same market. Its effects are that:
- economies of scale are likely, though diseconomies are possible due to poor communications and coordination
- there is an increased market share and reduction in competition, though there are possible monopoly issues if market share reaches 25%

Conglomerate

This describes integration between firms operating in unrelated markets. Its effects are that:
- diversification helps to spread risk
- there is a sharing of good practice, but management may have no expertise in the new business field

Remember that demergers also occur, often as a result of unsuccessful takeovers and the subsequent need for companies to focus more clearly on their core activities.

Management buyouts

This is where management buys the company it runs; it is the takeover of a business or division of a business by its existing management team. Finance comes variously from managers' personal funds, loans and investments, or selling shares to employees.

Reasons for buyouts
- A large business might sell off a small section to raise cash, refocus the business

or get rid of an unprofitable section. The management team of the parent company's unwanted section might feel it could be successful with a different approach or more finance.

- Owners of a family business who wish to retire might prefer to sell to the management team in the hope of maintaining employment and continuity.
- The firm might be in the hands of the receiver, who must try to keep it going in order to raise money to pay off creditors. One way of doing this is to sell part of it to the management team.

Rewards of buyouts

- Management and employees have more motivation and personal responsibility.
- Objectives may be clearer because there is no owner/manager conflict.
- There is likely to be less bureaucracy in the form of a head office that might hinder progress.
- There is no possibility that profits will be diverted to another part of the organisation.
- If successful, the possibility exists of floating the company on the stock market or selling shares in a takeover offer.

Risks of buyouts

- If unsuccessful, personal losses are felt by the new owners or investors.
- The original owners might have been correct in assessing that the business was fundamentally unprofitable.
- There may be little access to capital.
- They often involve considerable rationalisation and job losses, with adverse effects on staff morale.

Analysis Opportunities for analysis of changes in ownership include:
- assessing the implications for a firm of organic growth compared to external growth
- examining the motives for the various types of external growth available to a firm
- considering the risks and rewards for management and for the workforce that might result from a management buyout

Evaluation Opportunities for evaluation include:
- assessing why a business might do better if it is run as a management buyout rather than if it is run by the same management team as part of a larger plc
- evaluating the extent to which stakeholder groups other than the management team benefit from a management buyout
- assessing the reasons for and against growth by means of takeover

Links Possible links to other areas include operations management in relation to economies and diseconomies of scale, people in relation to motivation, and management style.

Business objectives

Revise the material on mission statements, corporate aims and objectives, and stake-holders and their common and conflicting aims covered in AS Unit 3.

Mission and organisational culture

Mission statement

A mission statement contains the ultimate reason for an organisation's existence, thus providing employees with a justification for their work. In this sense it can shape the corporate culture. The values in a mission statement should reflect the most commonly held beliefs and assumptions among employees that might already form an unwritten code known as the organisational culture. The code influences employees' attitudes, their approach to management and their understanding of how decisions are made. If employees can feel proud of the set of values, this in turn motivates them to work towards the organisation's objectives.

Organisational culture

The culture of an organisation reflects its objectives, decision-making and behaviour. The sources of organisational culture are as follows:
- company routines — the way everyday decisions and tasks are undertaken
- formal controls — the rules and procedures governing employee actions
- organisational structures — the way management is organised
- power structure — the relationship between individuals and the groups which take decisions and how the organisation's resources are allocated
- symbols — the forms of language used, plus signs of status such as pay, size and location of offices

Types of organisational culture

Power

This is where a powerful individual or a small group determines the dominant culture. In a small company, the founder determines the way the organisation operates. In some large companies, such as Virgin, a charismatic leader like Richard Branson does much to define the culture.

Role

Role-type cultures occur in bureaucracies that are governed by rules and procedures rather than by the values of particular individuals.

Task

This is where the organisation's values are related to a job or project. The emphasis is on the group through teamwork and adaptability.

Person

This occurs in the professions (accountancy and legal firms) where organisations exist as a vehicle for people to develop their own careers and expertise.

Bureaucratic culture

Examples of bureaucratic organisations are government departments, universities, banks and building societies. Their characteristics include:

- emphasis on roles and procedures (like role culture)
- risk avoidance
- generalised and non-commercial goals
- responsibilities and roles precisely defined
- a hierarchical structure
- people unsuited to a dynamic environment
- a culture where making the right decision is less important than making decisions the right way
- low business mortality, i.e. they tend to survive for long periods of time

Entrepreneurial culture

Entrepreneurial organisations are found in smaller businesses, profit-centred organisations and conglomerates with local management control. The characteristics of an entrepreneurial culture include:

- emphasis on results
- reward for individual initiative (like power culture)
- risk-taking
- quantitative, especially financial, goals
- a task culture with flexible roles
- a flatter and more flexible structure, more local control
- commercial results, profits and loss
- high business mortality

   Analysis Opportunities for analysis of business culture include:
   - considering the different types of organisational culture and how these might influence an organisation's decision-making
   - examining the purpose of an organisation's mission statement

   Evaluation Opportunities for evaluation include:
   - discussing to what extent the culture of an organisation might impede its ability to change in the future
   - assessing the extent to which it is difficult to change organisational culture
   - evaluating the extent to which an organisation's culture might influence its decision-making
   - judging how useful mission statements are for an organisation

   Links Possible links to other areas include corporate aims and goals, short- and long-term objectives, and conflicting and common goals of stakeholders.

Business strategy

Decision-making to achieve objectives

Decision-making models

Decision-making in any business is very important. Types of decision vary, as do the people who make them. Decisions are usually constrained in some way by both internal and external factors. A number of decision-making models are available to assist firms in this difficult and important process.

The marketing model

This is an example of a scientific approach to decision-making and involves the following stages:

- reviewing the current position and evaluating past performance
- setting objectives for the future
- gathering data needed to inform the decision
- analysing the data and finding out what they mean
- selecting a strategy and deciding what shall be done
- developing a strategic plan, which identifies how to achieve objectives
- reviewing the outcome and evaluating performance in relation to objectives

Ansoff's matrix

This is another decision-making model or tool for corporate planning that provides a range of strategic options, each with a different degree of risk attached.

In looking at the strategic options available in Ansoff's matrix, remember to draw upon your understanding across all of the functional areas and the external influences. Try to take an integrative view of business when using this model.

Existing products, existing markets

This is a low-risk strategy, where the company has a choice of whether to:
- penetrate the market further, for example by increasing brand loyalty
- consolidate its present position by concentrating on maintaining market share
- withdraw from the market altogether if there is an irreversible decline in demand
- do nothing, which might be appropriate in the short term but not in the long term

Existing products, new markets

Here the strategy of market development is followed to extend market penetration into fresh areas. Examples are new geographical territories, new uses being promoted for the product, or entering new market segments.

New products, existing markets

Here a product development strategy is followed, which may involve substantial modifications or additions to a product range. However, the company operates from the security of its established customers.

New products, new markets

This is a high-risk strategy. Diversification could involve a move into new but related markets by vertical or horizontal integration, or into new and unrelated markets by conglomerate integration.

Analysis Opportunities for analysis of decision-making include:
- considering the implications of a company moving from its existing product and existing market to a new product and new market
- examining the various stages involved in a scientific decision-making model such as the marketing model

Evaluation Opportunities for evaluation include:
- judging which strategic option (from Ansoff's matrix) a risk-averse firm is likely to follow and why
- evaluating the extent to which decision-making models assist firms in achieving objectives

Links Possible links include marketing in relation to marketing mix and marketing strategy, objectives and strategy in relation to methods of growth (horizontal, vertical and conglomerate), and operations management in relation to research and development.

Decision trees

Constructing a decision tree

Decision trees are diagrams that set out all the options available when making a decision, plus the outcomes that might result by chance. They are usually helpful where a sequence of events or options has to be followed in conditions of uncertainty. However, as with all quantitative models, caution must be exercised when considering the nature of the information used and the results themselves.

Stages in constructing a decision tree:
- identify the options available to the business
- assess the likely outcomes of each of these options
- attach probabilities to each option available to the firm
- estimate the likely financial returns from each option identified
- calculate the expected value of each option
- choose the option generating the highest expected value

Ensure that you feel confident in calculating percentages and the expected value of an outcome; always include all of your workings when answering questions on this area.

An example of a decision tree is shown below.

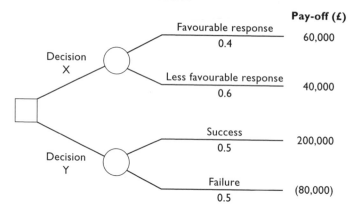

Expected value of X = (0.4 × 60,000) + (0.6 × 40,000)

= 24,000 + 24,000 = 48,000

Expected value of Y = (0.5 × 200,000) + (0.5 × 80,000)

= 100,000 + (40,000) = 60,000

Y has the highest expected value, but it has a 50:50 chance of generating a loss.

Advantages of using decision trees

- They encourage a careful consideration of all alternatives.
- They set out a problem clearly and encourage a logical approach to decision-making.
- They encourage a quantitative consideration of chance.
- They help to take risk into account when making decisions.
- They are useful in tactical or routine decisions rather than strategic decisions.
- They discourage gut-reaction decision-making.

Disadvantages of using decision trees

- It is hard to get accurate or meaningful data for probabilities.
- They are less useful in the case of new problems or one-off strategic problems.
- It is easy for management bias to occur because a manager can manipulate the data.
- They ignore changes in the business environment that affect the outcome of decisions.
- They may lead to managers taking less account of qualitative issues.

Ensure that you understand the procedures to use and how to calculate decision trees. Equally, if not more importantly, ensure that you understand the shortcomings of the method and the fact that qualitative factors involved in any decision must not be ignored simply because the numbers look convincing.

Analysis Opportunities for analysing decision trees include:
- considering how important factors other than the results of a decision tree exercise might be
- analysing the advantages and disadvantages of using decision trees as a tool

Evaluation Opportunities for evaluation include:
- assessing the important issues that should be taken into account when using decision trees to assist in decision-making
- evaluating the overall effectiveness of using decision trees in a new market

Links Possible links could be made to functional areas and external influences in order to take an integrative approach when considering decision-making.

Corporate plan (medium to long term)

As with all areas in this module, this topic is linked with other parts of the specification, drawing upon the knowledge and understanding gained across the functional areas, external influences and other aspects of objectives and strategy.

Strategic planning

Once aims and objectives have been decided, a firm needs to draw up a plan of action detailing how these will be achieved. The plan should cover both medium- and long-term actions and is known as the firm's corporate or business strategy. The strategic planning process involves the stages outlined below.

Mission statement
This sets out the purpose of the organisation and its corporate aims.

Objectives
This stage breaks down the corporate aims and indicates how they can be achieved in terms of functional objectives.

Internal environment

This assesses the organisation's core competencies, what its key resources are and how successful it is in its markets.

External environment

This assesses the key changes that are taking place in the organisation's external environment.

SWOT analysis

This identifies the key internal strengths and weaknesses of the organisation and the external opportunities and threats, suggesting what the organisation needs to do to counter threats, to seize opportunities, to build on its strengths and to overcome its weaknesses.

Strategic choice

This identifies a range of options available to the organisation using, for example, Ansoff's matrix.

Strategic implementation

This puts a strategy into effect, creating a framework and responsibility for carrying out the strategy at a functional or departmental level.

Control

This monitors and reviews the success of the strategy.

Evaluation

This assesses actual performance compared to what was intended. It enables modifications to be made to the mission/aim and to the objectives, SWOT analysis, strategic choices and implementation strategies. It is therefore not only a control device but also a means of continuous improvement.

Revise the section on SWOT analysis and business strategy in the AS Module 3/AS Unit 3 guide. Ensure that you read a newspaper or listen to the news regularly so that you are able to identify the dynamic nature of the external environment and to note changes taking place within it.

Analysis Opportunities for analysis of corporate planning include:
- examining how aims and objectives are translated into actions
- explaining why a firm might need to modify its planning process

Evaluation Opportunities for evaluation include:
- assessing the extent to which a corporate plan helps a firm to pursue its objectives
- judging the circumstances in which a firm might ignore these procedures

Links Possible links to other areas include an integrated approach to general issues covered in marketing, accounting and finance, people, operations management, external influences and SWOT analysis.

Contingency planning

Crises

A crisis is any unexpected event that threatens the well-being or survival of a brand or a whole firm and is dealt with by crisis management. It is important to distinguish situations that are real crises from those that are fairly predictable and quantifiable risks that can be dealt with by contingency planning. This is the difference, say, between fluctuations in exchange rates and natural disasters. Like any other form of insurance, contingency planning reduces risk, but may seem like a waste of money if nothing ultimately goes wrong.

Effects of a crisis

Crises can have effects on marketing, finance, operations and personnel aspects of a business, and each function needs to be able to respond and manage the situation.

Marketing
When a firm's public image is under threat, successful public relations often forms a major part of managing a crisis.

Finance
Most crisis management requires immediate cash expenditure, whether on advertising campaigns, environmental clean-up campaigns or responding to hostile takeover bids.

Operations
Contingency planning is important in this area, especially if the company is reliant on just-in-time production systems.

Personnel
A crisis usually requires direct, authoritarian-type leadership in order to issue instructions and make quick decisions. In addition, effective internal and external communication systems are required. Internal communication should be direct, rapid and open; external communication should be informative, truthful and controlled.

Contingency planning

Contingency planning involves the following steps:
- recognising the need for it
- listing all possible crisis scenarios using 'what if' and sensitivity analysis
- searching for ways to prevent each crisis, for example by using extra quality checks, or relying less on a single supplier/buyer
- formulating crisis plans including the necessary human, financial and physical resources
- simulating crises and the operation of a contingency plan using software or actual exercises

Contingency planning versus crisis management

Contingency planning differs from crisis management in that it:

- prepares for predictable and quantifiable crises
- plans for unexpected and (usually) unwelcome events
- prepares for events that the organisation may have weeks to respond to
- uses computer models that provide systematic opportunities to ask and answer 'what if' questions
- gathers detailed information on predictable situations

Crisis management differs from contingency planning in that it:

- responds to a sudden event that poses a significant threat to a firm
- limits damage
- emphasises the need for a flexible response to any situation
- selects a crisis team to deal with any crises

Analysis Opportunities for analysis include:

- considering the various steps involved in contingency planning
- examining the differences between contingency planning and crisis management
- analysing how the various internal functions of a firm need to be able to respond to a crisis

Evaluation Opportunities for evaluation include:

- discussing to what extent a firm should deal differently with a real crisis compared to a fairly predictable and quantifiable risk
- judging whether, because things rarely go wrong, contingency planning is simply a waste of money

Links Possible links to other areas include marketing in relation to public relations, accounting and finance in relation to financial management, operations management in relation to JIT, and people in relation to leadership styles and communication systems.

Questions
&
Answers

There are six case studies in this section. Each case study is followed by two sample answers interspersed with examiner's comments.

Questions

The questions are based on the format of the A2 papers. Unit 6 (External Influences and Objectives and Strategy) differs from Units 4 and 5 in that greater weighting is given to evaluation. Most questions, therefore, carry more marks for evaluation than the other skills of knowledge, application and analysis.

Tackle the questions in this book to develop your technique, allowing yourself 90 minutes to answer all parts of each question. The specimen answers and examiner's comments show how these questions can best be answered and how to avoid making inappropriate responses during the exam.

A common problem for students (and teachers) when completing a topic is the lack of examination questions that cover only that topic. These questions have been tailored so that students can apply their learning whilst a topic is still fresh in their minds. Questions 1 to 5 are focused on a specific area of content covered in the same order as the Content Guidance section of this guide. These questions may be tackled during the course, or on completion of the revision of that particular content area. Question 6 is integrated, with a weighting towards business strategy. Remember, you will be given credit for using business concepts from outside a unit, as long as their inclusion and use is relevant to the question. This is particularly important in Unit 6, which is the synoptic unit.

Sample answers

Resist the temptation to study the answers before you have attempted the questions. In each case, the first answer (by candidate A) is intended to show the type of response that would earn an A-grade on that paper. An A-grade does not mean perfection — these answers show the range of responses that can earn high marks. In business studies, it is the quality of the reasoning that is rewarded. Candidate B's answers demonstrate responses that warrant a pass, but not at grade A.

Examiner's comments

The examiner's comments are preceded by the icon *e*. They are interspersed in the answers and indicate where credit is due. In the weaker answers, the comments point out areas for improvement, specific problems and common errors.

Q uestion 1

Economic opportunities and constraints

Executive Trading Ltd

Executive Trading Ltd is a producer of executive toys, gifts and accessories that has been trading successfully for about 5 years within the UK. It is a relatively small firm employing 250 people in a factory in North Staffordshire. The products are assembled or finished here, basic production being done cheaply in southeast Asia and then bought in. Products are sold as generic items or, more usually, customised with the purchaser's logo. Big companies are the main customers.

Sue Chester (the managing director and finance director) and Joe Stockton (the marketing and operations director) have been discussing the possibility of exporting to German and US markets. As somebody who is averse to taking risks, Sue anticipates overwhelming problems. Joe, on the other hand, is very keen and sees few problems.

At a local Chamber of Commerce lunch held in honour of a group of overseas business people, Sue and Joe got into discussion with an American and a German, both of whom felt there were opportunities for Executive Trading in their countries. The four agreed to discuss this further over lunch the following day. The lunch went well, with Sue and Joe being invited to visit their new friends in Germany and the US.

'Many US companies give away Executive Trading-type gifts at conferences, to their staff and as general give-aways,' the American said. He also suggested that such products are relatively price-inelastic — because they represent such a small cost to the buying firm — and thus would be unaffected by the strength of the pound. The German was more cautious. While he recognised there probably were opportunities in Germany for Executive Trading products, he was more concerned about the problems of trading within Europe, given that Britain had not adopted the euro. He noted that his own firm had decided that it would no longer contract with UK firms unless all transactions were in euros.

'Let's go for it,' Joe said after the meeting.

Sue remained cautious. 'I'm not convinced our products are price-inelastic,' she said. 'There are always other firms trying to get a toehold in the market and prepared to suffer a loss or just break even to grab a contract. And what about our production capacity? If we get new contracts, we've got to deliver. What about our suppliers?'

Joe pointed out that Executive Trading could get supplies from any number of other firms if the existing one couldn't cope. 'Anyway the strong pound is good for us in terms of our suppliers and our costs,' he said. 'And don't forget that we might be able to cut costs further if we can generate some economies of scale.'

Sue remained sceptical. 'With the US likely to go into recession, surely this isn't the right time to try to enter the market.' 'Recession isn't bad for every firm,' Joe countered. 'We'll need more staff,' said Sue. 'We'll get them,' said Joe. 'Where from? Our factory is hardly in the most populated area of the country, is it? What if we need extra capacity?'

Joe had a ready answer. 'I've been thinking about that,' he said. 'The site next door is available for sale. We could put in an offer and consider expansion.' When Sue enquired about the cost, Joe reassured her that interest rates were low and added: 'You're always telling me we're a really low-geared company.'

'You know how cautious I am,' Sue replied. 'Any risk and I start to worry, but I don't want to ignore a good opportunity. Let's take up the offer of our American and German friends. One week in each country to investigate the market and then we'll make a decision — promise.'

(1) Joe suggested that interest rates were low. How might this fact influence a decision to enter new markets abroad? (14 marks)

(2) Assess the implications of a strong pound on Executive Trading's ability to enter the US market. (14 marks)

(3) In relation to Executive Trading, evaluate Joe's comment that not all businesses are adversely affected by recession. (16 marks)

(4) To what extent can the internal aspects of a firm such as production, people, marketing and strategic issues determine how competitive Executive Trading might be if it entered the US and/or German markets? (18 marks)

(5) Discuss the extent to which non-membership of the euro will influence the competitiveness of UK firms in Europe and assess how Executive Trading might overcome any problems. (18 marks)

Total: 80 marks

■ ■ ■

Answer to question 1: candidate A

(1) Interest rates are the price of money, whether borrowing or lending. If interest rates are low, this should have a number of effects on Executive Trading Ltd's decision to enter new markets.

💡 It is always good to start by defining terms.

Low interest rates make investment more attractive and reduce business costs. Joe mentioned the site next door, which could be purchased more cheaply with a loan when interest rates are low. This would allow them room for the expansion they might need in order to enter new markets. The fact that costs can be kept down might help them to price competitively, which would be very important in terms of gaining a foothold in a new market.

💡 The effect of low interest rates and the explanation of it are focused on the question and provide good analysis and application to the situation.

Low interest rates are said to benefit highly geared firms by reducing the interest payments, but they are also of benefit if a company wishes to expand by taking on more loans. So although Executive Trading is a low-geared company it could still benefit from low interest rates.

✍ This relates well to the context and shows judgement, especially in recognising that Executive Trading's situation is likely to change.

Low interest rates in the longer term might lead to a fall in the value of the pound. This would then make exports more competitive, which would certainly help in the US market. However, the text suggests that Executive Trading's products might be price-inelastic, and this makes low interest rates less important. Because of the euro, it is less clear what effects a fall in the pound would have on the German market.

✍ The last sentence needs some explanation, but otherwise good analysis and evaluation are shown here. Note how the application of the answer to the situation is helping candidate A to evaluate.

The fact that the products it sells are likely to be price-inelastic, and the fact that the low interest rates are in the UK and therefore don't affect consumers in either the US or Germany, mean there is likely to be little effect on the demand side. The main effect is likely to be in terms of the cost of loans and therefore the cost of any investment, such as buying the site next door in order to expand to meet capacity needs for the new market.

✍ The comment about the effect on demand shows a clear understanding of the situation and is a mature judgement.

(2) A strong pound means that the exchange rate of the pound to the dollar is high, e.g. £1 = $3 rather than £1 = $1.5. A strong pound makes exports more expensive and imports cheaper; therefore if Executive Trading tries to sell in the American market, its prices will be higher than they might have been if the pound had been lower. This is the simple explanation. However, other things are important.

✍ This is a clear explanation with recognition that the analysis is more complex than basic theory suggests.

Whether export prices are considered high depends on the prices of similar goods in the US. If the US has high inflation, Executive Trading's exports — even with a strong pound — may still be competitive. If US inflation is low, this will simply make Executive Trading even less price-competitive.

✍ Excellent analysis is provided here. Candidate A recognises that the pound is not the only significant factor.

Products that are price-inelastic should not suffer too much from a strong pound because demand is not very responsive to price changes. So if price goes up because of the pound, demand will hardly fall at all. In the text, the US salesman says Executive Trading's products are inelastic, but Sue is not convinced about this. She thinks there are too many substitutes available, making her products elastic. Another issue is that it depends on whether Executive Trading wants to reduce its profit margins. Even if the pound is strong, export prices don't have to rise if the exporter decides to keep prices stable and reduce profit margins.

✎ The candidate analyses clearly two more interesting and relevant points.

All in all, the price-inelasticity of Executive Trading's products will determine whether or not a strong pound makes any difference. I think they are price-inelastic, although they are probably income-elastic too. When firms suffer reduced income/profit they will probably dispense with these goods, but if income/profits are good they will buy large quantities. Executive Trading probably wouldn't want to cut profit margins, certainly not when entering the market for the first time and — given Sue's attitude to risk — this would affect their willingness rather than their ability to enter.

✎ This is a good analysis with sound judgement based on the situation and the information available. The candidate is benefiting from close reading of the text, the importance of which students often underestimate.

(3) Depending on the nature of the products sold, some firms may be more affected by different phases of the business cycle, such as recession, than others. A recession is usually defined as a period when gross domestic product has been falling for two quarters in a row. This means income will also be falling. So firms that are selling income-elastic goods will suffer the most. A construction company selling houses will suffer a lot compared to a toothpaste seller.

✎ This opening paragraph demonstrates a clear understanding of the terms and recognition of the direction of the question, although the final sentence should have been justified.

Executive Trading could be affected by recession in both the UK and the USA if it enters the US market. Because of falling incomes, firms tend not to enter into investment projects during recession due to uncertainty about whether the economy will pick up. Sue and Joe might therefore be a bit wary of getting a loan to buy the new site.

✎ This is a useful issue to consider that is relevant to the situation and shows judgement.

Unemployment usually rises during a recession, which in turn affects people's income and their demand for goods. The real issue here is whether Executive Trading's products are income-inelastic. The text suggests they might or might not be and Sue thinks they are not. But in a recession, prices don't tend to rise so that isn't important. It does say that Executive Trading-type products 'represent such a small cost to the buying firm'. This might mean they are also income-inelastic, so when income/profit falls, firms will just keep buying because the amount paid is too small to notice. On the other hand, it could mean that if income/profit falls, firms will decide to cut back on all the extras, which is what these products are. Joe doesn't see this as a problem, so he must think Executive Trading products are income-inelastic. I tend to agree with this. If firms are doing badly because of recession, withdrawing their corporate accessories is unlikely to compensate for falling demand.

Z Here we see convincing evaluation based on the candidate's own analysis and information from the text. The application of theory from AS Module 1 (elasticity of demand) enhances the answer (although credit would still be given if the candidate had merely used the logic shown without using the concept of elasticity).

(4) To be competitive in foreign markets, Executive Trading really needs to be price-competitive. This will depend to some extent on external factors like inflation rates and the strength of the pound. It will also depend on Executive Trading's costs. If it can keep costs down this should help. Joe seems to think that they might be able to generate economies of scale if they expanded, which would reduce unit costs.

Z This is not a particularly strong start. It mentions a number of important issues and shows some judgement but lacks structure, which may affect the rest of the answer.

The question is also about Executive Trading's efficiency and productiveness. This might mean looking at production processes and possibly introducing new technology, or looking at staffing and the skills of employees. Sue thinks they might not have enough skilled staff if the company expands. Another issue is the strategic decision of whether Executive Trading should expand and how. Marketing will be really important. It must get foreign firms interested and this will be hard. The products will need a USP, whether it is price, quality or something else. This is especially true if there are lots of competitors.

Z This is much better. It considers the sort of internal factors that might affect competitiveness; it also contains some judgement.

Overall, being competitive abroad depends on getting all these internal issues right. It also depends on external factors such as the strength of the pound and inflation rates here and abroad since these could cancel out internal efforts.

Z Judgement is shown here in weighing up issues but there is no analysis or explanation of why external factors might cancel out internal efforts. It is also worth noting that external factors can be helpful too.

(5) The euro is a single currency adopted by 11 EU countries in 1999, which became fully operational by 2002.

Z This is a clear statement demonstrating knowledge.

Companies in countries with the euro will be able to trade with each other without any exchange rate transaction costs. This will save them money. UK firms, however, will still have to convert their currency, adding to their costs and perhaps their export prices, so making them less competitive. Exchange fluctuations between the pound and the euro will continue. So although firms in the euro zone will not have this problem, UK firms may still be influenced by (say) a strong pound in relation to the euro, again perhaps causing export prices to rise. One of the advantages to consumers of a single currency is price transparency, which is being able to compare prices easily. This won't be the case with a UK firm's products, and consumers may turn to European firms instead.

> Relevant issues are raised in the last paragraph; the analysis and evaluation are accurate but could be developed further.

Despite this, a lot of the papers are suggesting that even if we aren't in the euro, most UK firms doing business with Europe will start to do all their transactions in euros in order not to be disadvantaged.

> This is a good point which demonstrates wider reading.

How could Executive Trading overcome such problems? It could use spot and forward markets to guard against currency fluctuations. It might be better if it produced price lists and other marketing literature in euros and ensured that all transactions and dealings with potential German customers are in euros. This would also mean everything was set up if it wanted to expand into other European countries.

> This addresses the last part of the question well and relates to the problems considered in the first part.

> **Overall, this script is clearly A-grade standard. The candidate constantly focuses on the questions and uses information from the text well. In almost every question there is convincing judgement based on sound analysis together with clear knowledge and understanding of theory and concepts.**

■ ■ ■

Answer to question 1: candidate B

(1) If interest rates are low this should have certain effects on business.

> This is a worrying response which does not answer the question.

Saving is less attractive, so consumers might be spending more money. Depending on the nature of the product, this might mean more demand and thus a more optimistic view of the market being considered. But the fact that savings are less attractive is probably not relevant to Executive Trading Ltd, which sells most of its goods to companies and not individuals.

> This discussion demonstrates knowledge and some analysis and evaluation. The fact that the effect is not relevant to the company doesn't make it a bad point. However, it is not sufficiently focused on the question.

If it gets cheap loans and expands, this might lead to economies of scale, allowing unit costs to fall.

✍ A valid point, but it doesn't relate interest rates to new markets and is therefore not particularly useful unless it can be developed and explained fully.

Low interest rates are good for highly geared firms. Executive Trading is low geared so it is unlikely to benefit from them.

✍ This is not really the case and shows an overly simplistic view and a failure to relate to the question.

The cost of goods bought on credit will fall, meaning more demand for those goods. If Executive Trading's goods are bought on credit, this will mean more demand.

✍ What about the question? The points made are correct, but how do they apply to Executive Trading and its desire to enter a new market? Always answer the question set: there is nothing to be gained by answering the question that you wanted the examiner to set (unless it is the question that was set).

(2) A strong pound is where the value of the pound in terms of the dollar is good.

✍ It's good that a definition of terms has been attempted, but this is a bit vague.

It usually means that exports rise in price and imports fall in price. So if exports go up in price, demand for them will fall. This means Executive Trading will receive less money. If imports fall in price, Executive Trading's imported stocks/components will be cheaper so its costs will fall and may make products cheaper. This might cancel out the increase in price due to the strong pound.

✍ The information is accurate and demonstrates some analysis but it could have been written without having read the text. It is over-simplistic and does not consider any relevant issues from the text.

(3) Recession is part of the business cycle and is when incomes are falling. Falling income leads to falling demand, unemployment and output and eventually income, which again leads to falling demand and so on. So Executive Trading will be hit by a fall in demand for its products, which could have serious effects on its profits eventually.

✍ There is nothing wrong with the information in this answer — the theory and analysis of consequences are accurate — but the question has, in fact, been ignored.

(4) Internal factors like those mentioned in the question are important. Marketing needs to be right, production needs to be efficient and of quality, and workers need to be up to the job. But it's really about having the right price and making the right contacts. External factors could also be important.

✍ This is a weak response that is brief and lacks any analysis. A number of relevant issues are raised but not developed at all.

(5) The euro is a single currency. For companies in those countries that have introduced it, there will be no more exchange changes. So if they trade within this area there will be no more problems about a strong or weak currency. Also there will be no more costs involved in changing money from one currency to another. Customers will be able to compare prices easily. The UK's non-membership means that none of these advantages apply to UK firms so they will be left out.

 All of this is accurate, but the question itself is not specifically addressed other than in the last sentence, which is unsatisfactory.

Executive Trading should concentrate on the US and ignore Europe until the UK joins the euro.

 This is a very disappointing response to the last part of the question and suggests a reluctance to think through possible actions.

 In each of these answers, the candidate demonstrates understanding of concepts and theory. In general, the analysis, though often brief, is correct. However, the answers fail to address the questions posed and there is little application or evaluation in relation to Executive Trading. The answers could often have been written without having read the text. On this basis, the candidate would only achieve a borderline D grade.

Governmental opportunities and constraints

The bus business

Joe Townie was reflecting on his years in the transport business. He could go as far back as the mid-1970s when he was a bus driver, but he couldn't remember whether the buses then were either a sort of nationalised industry or were run by the local council. He was sure, however, that private sector companies hadn't been running them. He could remember when the Conservative government came to power in 1979 and the subsequent introduction of privatisation and deregulation. That was when things started looking up for him financially. He'd always wanted to work for himself, and the government's policy of deregulating the bus industry and opening it up to competition gave him the opportunity to start his own small bus company in his local area.

This had involved a huge amount of research to produce the information for the business plan and to obtain the financial support he needed. With hindsight, he thought that local people had been better served by his and a number of other competing bus companies. On the whole, he felt that privatisation and deregulation had been good moves, especially when he thought of the state of the service and the lack of incentive to change in the bus industry before this.

Despite some local competition, Joe's business had done very well; in fact the competition seemed a good thing, keeping them all on their toes. But then slowly everything began to change. Throughout the country a few large bus companies seemed to be either buying out small local companies or, where the small companies were unwilling to sell, setting up locally and fixing prices way below what small companies could compete with. When it began to happen in Joe's region, he saw what was coming and decided to sell out. He struck a reasonable deal that provided him with the financial security he needed for retirement. Most other local firms did the same. The few that decided to stay and fight were unsuccessful and eventually closed.

Iain, Joe's 17-year-old grandson, had been complaining about the fact that there were too few buses to take him from his rural home and into town. Joe pointed out how things had changed in the industry over the last 30 years and — to his amazement — Iain had been quite interested. Apparently Iain was studying A-level business studies and the discussions with his granddad had given him an idea for a coursework topic.

'It seems to me that, like everything else, things have moved full circle,' Joe said. 'When I worked as a bus driver, there was a single bus company operating in the area; then later there were quite a few small and competing companies; and now we're back, more or less, to a single company operating again.'

Iain replied that Joe's description of the bus industry provided a good example of the effects of intervention versus laissez-faire government policies. Joe was a bit confused with these

question

terms but on learning that laissez-faire meant 'relying on the discipline of the market' he recalled Margaret Thatcher, the Conservative prime minister of the 1980s, using the term often to justify her privatisation and deregulation policies.

Joe and Iain moved on to discuss how the bus industry had responded to changing government policy. Iain asked Joe whether he had any idea how the government's monetary policy had affected the performance of his bus company. Joe understood that this basically meant how interest rate changes had affected him and told Iain about his initial investment in buses and a small depot. Iain said that the effects were much broader than that and wanted to know how interest rates had affected his customers and suppliers and other groups. Joe was unsure about this and referred Iain to an article he'd been reading in the morning newspaper. It was all about interest rates, time lags and something called the multiplier effects and business.

Iain said that macroeconomic factors like levels of inflation, unemployment and economic growth could all affect a business and that government policies introduced to influence these factors would, in turn, affect business. His granddad's reminiscences confirmed the theory. 'When I was a driver, far fewer people had cars and there was a lot of unemployment so the buses were always full. These days buses appear fairly empty, and it seems to me to be mainly elderly and young people who travel on them.'

The discussion left Iain with a greater appreciation that all these macroeconomic factors are interrelated. He decided that it needed really careful thought to decide whether a particular government policy was an opportunity or a constraint, and that it must be difficult being chancellor of the exchequer, trying to juggle all these different demands.

(1) Joe mentions that the effects of government policy on business might be subject to time lags and multiplier effects. Assess the extent to which the effects of monetary and fiscal policy on business might be subject to such factors. (14 marks)

(2) Taking the bus industry as one example, and other examples of your choice, discuss how the impact of monetary and fiscal policy might differ depending on the nature of a business and its products. (14 marks)

(3) Evaluate the advantages and disadvantages to business of intervention versus laissez-faire government policies. (16 marks)

(4) To what extent might deregulation have benefited bus users in particular and the bus industry in general? (18 marks)

(5) Discuss the extent to which privatisation has opened industry up to the discipline of the market and improved efficiency. (18 marks)

Total: 80 marks

■ ■ ■

Answer to question 2: candidate A

(1) Fiscal and monetary policy are two ways in which the government can influence the economy. Fiscal policy is really using the budget and changes in taxation and government spending. Monetary policy is about changing interest rates;

this is now the responsibility of the Bank of England's Monetary Policy Committee. Both fiscal and monetary policy are used to change the level of demand in the economy. This will affect the demand for a firm's goods and in turn will affect how much it produces, how many workers it needs, the prices it charges etc.

☑ Candidate A makes an excellent start, demonstrating a clear understanding of the policies.

The extent to which this process is affected by time lags and the multiplier effect varies. For example, if the Bank of England reduces interest rates in order to encourage demand and prevent recession, this doesn't mean the average firm will get a boost in demand the next day. It depends on the type of goods it sells. If it sells cars and large goods that people often buy on credit, it might affect them fairly quickly. But, for a bus company, demand won't be affected much at all. However, its ability to invest in new capital goods will change as soon as interest rates change and its costs may increase if it has existing loans. Increasing demand might lead to more output as firms take on more workers who now have more money to spend and so on. This is the multiplier effect and after a time lag of, say, a year, some firms selling income-elastic goods may experience an increase in sales. The point is that it takes time for income to increase because the multiplier process takes time.

☑ This is a convincing discussion of how time lags and multiplier effects are important factors in the effect of interest rates on business.

Changes in government spending are the same. For example, building a new hospital means more demand for building work and all the other supplies needed as well as doctors and nurses and other staff. Overall, a lot more people are employed who have more money to spend and spend it locally so local businesses eventually do better.

☑ This paragraph discusses the effect of government spending on business and although it describes multiplier effects, it does not explicitly refer to any time lags.

Taxation changes can have fairly immediate impact though. If tax goes up, the price of tobacco, petrol and alcohol increases overnight. If the rate of income tax is slashed, then people immediately have more money to spend.

☑ Here time lags are explicitly covered but there is no indication of the impact of this on business.

None of this has much impact on the demand for bus journeys though, except that a hike in the price of petrol might stop people using their cars and switch to buses; but only if there is an efficient service with a good timetable.

☑ The conclusion, although related to the bus industry, is not really addressing the question, which is about the time lags and multiplier effects on business of changes to monetary and fiscal policy.

question

(2) The impact of changing interest rates (monetary policy) is unlikely to affect the demand for bus journeys, at least in the short term. It will, however, affect investment in buses and depots. High interest rates may deter firms taking out loans for these and might also increase the costs of a business that already has loans. This could increase prices. Indirectly, if high interest rates reduce the demand for cars (which are usually bought on credit), then they might lead to an increase in the demand for travel by bus. For something like cars or other products bought on credit, a change in interest rates can have an immediate effect on sales. It also means that for mortgage holders, disposable income changes. If interest rates increase, people have less money to spend and so demand — especially for luxury goods like new clothes and entertainment — might fall.

A change in income tax (fiscal policy) will have a direct effect on income. Bus journeys are probably not going to be affected by small changes in income, but a big fall in income tax might enable people to afford a car, which would have an effect on bus journeys. Government spending changes are unlikely to affect bus journeys but could mean more jobs and therefore more spending in a local area so supermarkets and other business will do better.

> ✐ These two paragraphs analyse clearly and effectively the possible effects of interest rates on the bus industry and other industries and their products, as requested by the question.

The effect of these policies is mainly on demand and therefore income, so generally it depends on whether the business sells income-elastic products. However, these policies also affect the ability to invest and costs, so it depends on the sort of market and competition the firm faces.

> ✐ The conclusion shows sound judgement and builds on the previous analysis, whilst also introducing an important concept — income elasticity of demand. Nonetheless, more could have been made of this idea.

(3) Intervention and laissez-faire government policies are essentially opposites. Laissez-faire means leave alone and is where a government plays little or no part in the economy, leaving things to the free market to determine. Prices are determined by supply and demand. The goods supplied depend on whether people want them and are prepared to pay for them, not whether they need them. Intervention means that government takes an active part in influencing how the economy performs. The sorts of intervention that can happen include influencing exchange rates, legislation to protect consumers and workers and competition policy to curb monopolies.

> ✐ This is an excellent introduction that demonstrates clear understanding of the policies under discussion.

The advantages of laissez-faire are that for business there is less regulation and interference, so business gets on with doing its job. There are fewer costs involved and less red tape to deal with, so business is more efficient, prices might be lower and consumers might get a better deal. On the other hand, workers might be exploited and paid low wages and given bad conditions, and consumers might be charged high prices for necessities.

Intervention assumes the government knows best and has a broader view of the needs of the whole economy. It also means that there is a more level playing field for firms to operate in. Powerful monopolies cannot do just what they want and small firms are protected. Workers and consumers are treated more fairly, so they cannot be exploited and paid low wages or charged high prices. But there might be lots of regulations and red tape to follow, and this increases costs and stifles initiative and enterprise.

☑ In these two paragraphs the candidate analyses advantages and disadvantages of both policies well.

In general, there are advantages and disadvantages to both systems. Perhaps the best situation is one with sufficient intervention to ensure workers and consumers are not exploited and firms are allowed to operate efficiently and enough laissez-faire to provide reasonable freedom of choice.

☑ This is a well-judged conclusion, which in this case is more effective than trying to argue for one policy rather than another.

(4) Deregulation of the bus industry meant allowing private bus companies to set up and sell their services. This meant a lot of competition, at least at first. Joe says competition kept them on their toes. This means that all the bus companies tried to provide as many services and routes as possible, at as low a price as possible and with as good quality buses and general customer relations as possible. This was bound to benefit consumers who were getting a better but cheaper service. It probably provided incentives for the bus companies to become more efficient in order to survive, given the competition. The problem was that gradually bigger companies started taking over the smaller ones or undercutting them to get rid of them. This was all right for the survivors but not for those that went under. It could be argued that this just got rid of the inefficient ones. As long as customer service didn't deteriorate this was probably true. But as you get fewer and larger bus companies they begin to have local monopolies, and if no one uses a particular route much they just chop it and consumers then begin to lose out.

☑ This is a convincing analysis and judgement of the impact of deregulation. Issues are dealt with clearly, and with examples based on customers and the bus industry the application is particularly effective.

The extent to which bus users have benefited is debatable and probably depends on the extent to which a local area is in the hands of a monopoly or not and, if so, how socially responsible the monopolist is. The bus industry in general is probably much more efficient, profitable and up to date. But without competition it probably won't remain so.

☑ The candidate draws an evaluative conclusion that has some merit and is based soundly on the foregoing analysis.

(5) Privatisation is the government selling off previously nationalised industries to the private sector with shares offered to the public. This happened to gas, water, electricity, railways etc. and meant competition in areas where there had been none before. The profit motive would lead to more efficiency, more choice, lower costs and lower prices. Everyone would seem to benefit.

✒ This is a good start, demonstrating understanding of the term and analysing the positive effects.

But many of these businesses were natural monopolies before, which means that the most efficient type of production was via a single firm. Over time there have been mergers and takeovers and many are monopolies again, although now in private hands. To control this, the government has introduced regulators like OFWAT to ensure that private companies don't exploit consumers or prevent competitive behaviour.

✒ Here the candidate takes a critical view of privatisation and is again able to quote examples and to explain clearly and succinctly.

So although privatisation opened up industry to the discipline of the market, the industries chosen are, to some extent, now private monopolies, which the government controls in a different way. But they are more profitable and more efficient because of the profit motive.

✒ This conclusion makes a reasoned judgement as to whether the statement in the question is true.

✒ **This is an A-grade script in which the candidate focuses on the question and uses information from the text. Some answers could have been developed further, but in almost every one there is reasoned and convincing judgement based on sound analysis. In every case, clear knowledge and understanding of theory and concepts are shown, providing an excellent basis for developing the answer.**

■ ■ ■

Answer to question 2: candidate B

(1) Monetary policy is changing interest rates. The government does this when it wants to reduce inflation. High interest rates mean people can't buy so much, so demand falls and prices stop rising. It could be used to prevent recession and encourage people to spend. This increases demand and so firms sell more, employ more people and generally do well.

✒ The candidate's answer is moving too quickly. In the second half it should have been noted that lower interest rates were in place. Try to make sure that your writing keeps in touch with your thinking.

Fiscal policy is tax and government expenditure. Taxation is a leakage from the economy and reduces spending and income. Government expenditure is an injection and increases spending and income.

☑ This includes reasonable explanation of the impact of fiscal policy on income and spending, but there is no mention of time lags or multiplier effects as required by the question.

Neither of them works straight away. Changes to government and taxes have to wait until they are announced in the budget. Interest rates have to wait for the chancellor to announce them. Interest rates usually change overnight and some taxes do too. Other taxes and government expenditure plans often happen at some future date.

☑ This shows that the candidate has not understood time lags and multiplier effects in the context of the question posed.

(2) Monetary policy means changing interest rates to check inflation. If inflation looks like going up, the interest rates will be raised. For the bus industry this will increase interest costs and might lead to increased prices. It might stop companies getting loans for further investment such as buses and depots.

☑ The analysis, although rather simple, demonstrates clearly the possible effects of changing interest rates on the bus industry. It does not, however, look at any other industry as requested by the question.

Changes in taxation like VAT will mean higher prices too. This will mean a fall in demand. Perhaps people will walk instead. Income tax increases will mean people have less money to spend and so will buy fewer bus journeys. If government spending increases, this might mean better roads and therefore more efficient bus journeys.

☑ The analysis here is too simplistic. More thought needs to be given to the consequences of changes in policies on the bus industry. Furthermore, no consideration is given to the consequences of changes in policies on other industries.

Therefore the impact of monetary and fiscal policy differs depending on the nature of the business and its products.

☑ The conclusion simply restates the question. Ensure that your conclusion adds to the earlier parts of your response.

(3) Laissez-faire means no government interference, so firms can do what they want and don't have lots of laws and regulations to constrain them. They can therefore make more profit. But this could mean monopolies grow and become more and more powerful, exploiting consumers, and no one can stop them. Intervention means that the government passes laws to protect consumers and workers and to constrain powerful firms and stop monopolies. This is good, but such laws can prevent initiative being taken and prevent competition, which brings efficiency and choice.

> Although brief, this answer does contain many of the important issues in the debate. It considers the advantages and disadvantages of both policies and some judgement is shown. There is, however, little analysis and therefore little material on which to base a judgement.

(4) Deregulation has meant a move from one government-owned company to loads of small competitors (which is how Joe got in) and then back to a single monopoly. Consumers are supposed to benefit from competition with more choice, lower prices and better services. This is what happened for customers using buses. Also, more competition forces firms to be more efficient if they want to stay in business. They have to keep costs down, introduce the latest technology and streamline themselves.

> Benefits to bus users and to the industry in general have been considered here. There is some fairly superficial analysis, but there is no judgement shown.

(5) Privatisation meant selling shares in previously public companies to the public, e.g. coal, steel and telephones. Competition was introduced and this led to more efficiency. If firms face competition, they have to make sure that they are as efficient as possible so that their costs (and thus prices) are as low as possible, and that their products are as high quality as possible. In this sense privatisation has opened industry up to the discipline of the market and improved efficiency. But the government has had to introduce regulation into these industries since privatisation through watchdogs such as OFTEL, and so it can't have worked that well.

> This answer contains some simple but relevant analysis. The last sentence could have been the basis of further analysis leading to evaluation. Instead, it was simply a statement.

> **With the exception of part 1, the candidate demonstrates understanding of concepts and theory and raises issues that are relevant. However, answers to parts 1 and 2 fail to address the questions posed fully and all answers contain insufficient analysis and very little evaluation. On this basis, the response would be awarded a D grade.**

Social and other opportunities and constraints

Carnbridge Chemicals

Dead fish were floating in a local lake, clouds of fumes hung low in the sky and Moira Donahue was livid.

'How can this possibly have happened?' she demanded. 'We've taken every precaution in the book and our whole mission is bound up in our ethical position and our safety-first policy.'

As managing director of Carnbridge Chemicals, Moira was facing the worst moment of her career. There had been a chemical leak in an area of outstanding natural beauty in the north-west of England during the main holiday season and everyone was saying the leak was from her company.

Moira and her team of senior managers were having an emergency breakfast meeting. Despite the early hour, the phones were red-hot with calls from environmental groups, the local and national media, and numerous local individuals affected by the leakage.

The operations manager, Tom Perks, said: 'I can't understand it either. There is absolutely no evidence in the plant of a leak. I've had the men checking all the possibilities and every-thing is as it should be. Like you say, we've always done our utmost to ensure there's no adverse environmental impact from our production process. I don't need to remind you that only last year we opted for a less profitable but much safer process in our new plant, one with no risk of leakage or contamination.'

The group remembered that decision. It had been a difficult one. A lengthy cost–benefit analysis had been commissioned at the suggestion of the finance director, Bill Leighton. Bill was, unusually for an accountant, keen on ensuring that external costs and benefits were taken into account in their decision-making. He had worked in the chemical industry all his life and had seen too many decisions taken on a purely financial basis sometimes with subse-quent disastrous results.

Sonia Westward, the marketing director with responsibility for public relations, said: 'We have to move on this. Whatever the cause, the finger is being pointed at us. The environ-mental pressure groups — with the help of the media — are going to have a field day and we have to decide how to respond. If we don't, they could close us down and we'll certainly forfeit good will in the area. At the very least, we'll lose business.'

The meeting continued with tense discussion back and forth. Moira pointed out that everyone assumed that Carnbridge — the only chemical manufacturer in the area — was the polluter. 'Tom,' she said, 'I want your team to spend the morning checking to see whether we are to blame in any way. We'll meet again at noon and decide our plans. Sonia, please draft a media statement to the effect that we don't believe the leak is down to us and we are investigating our own system to check this out.'

By 12.30 p.m., the management team was confident that Carnbridge Chemicals was not at fault. The local police, however, had discovered that empty drums with Carnbridge markings had been found on a lakeside. 'It might be relevant or it might just be gossip,' said Tom Perks, 'but one of the lads in the plant heard something suspicious last night. He was in his local pub and a group of three or four young people were asking all sorts of questions: who the main employers were in the area; what they did; how far they were from the nearest river. They were strangers to him. Later he saw these same young people in deep discussion. I know it's a long shot but this pollution could possibly have been a deliberate act by someone outside the company.'

The police were expected later that afternoon and the team decided it would be useful to mention its suspicion of sabotage to them. Meanwhile, Carnbridge gave the media its mission statement and independent social audit and anything else that could help persuade people of its reputation for safety, sound ethical behaviour and social responsibility. Moira set about organising public tours of the plant in an effort to counter the mounting pressure group activity and to re-establish her firm's reputation.

(1) **Evaluate the view that accepting social responsibility makes good business sense to an organisation such as Carnbridge Chemicals.** (14 marks)

(2) **The text suggests that Carnbridge Chemicals did not select the most profitable processing option available to it. To what extent could you argue that such ethical decision-making is profitable?** (14 marks)

(3) **Discuss the possible conflict between ethical decision-making and delegation. On the basis of evidence in the text, examine whether it is likely that such conflict exists at Carnbridge Chemicals.** (16 marks)

(4) **Assess the possible impact of pressure group activity on a firm such as Carnbridge Chemicals and how the firm should respond in order to minimise such impact.** (18 marks)

(5) **The text suggests that Carnbridge Chemicals has an independently produced social audit. Explain what a social audit involves and evaluate the benefits of social auditing to business organisations in general and to Carnbridge Chemicals in particular.** (18 marks)

Total: 80 marks

Answer to question 3: candidate A

(1) Social responsibilities are the duties that a firm owes to all its various stakeholders, not just shareholders but also employees, customers, suppliers and the local community and even the environment generally. It probably makes good business sense to accept these responsibilities. If the firm gets a good reputation for this,

it might mean it gets more customers who also stay loyal, motivation among the workforce might be better, and the local community might be more sympathetic to new developments.

All these things will help a company to increase sales and improve profits. This is especially true for a chemical company like Carnbridge that will need to get the local community on its side. It will have lorries congesting the roads in the rural northwest and unless people feel it is giving something back, that could give it a bad reputation.

> ✎ Starting with a definition of terms always helps an answer. The candidate then focuses directly on the question, demonstrating clear analysis and argument and relating this directly to Carnbridge Chemicals.

If Carnbridge was to ignore its social responsibilities then it might leave itself open to pressure group action from local groups or more organised environmental pressure groups. This seems to be happening in the case study, even though the company didn't ignore social responsibilities. But the public doesn't know that. Also, a company like Carnbridge Chemicals probably wouldn't get the loyal employees if it didn't have a good reputation.

> ✎ To evaluate a view requires a consideration of both sides of an argument, and here the candidate offers relevant discussion on the possible implications of ignoring social responsibility.

So, in general, I think it does make good business sense, but a company might have to prioritise sometimes or compromise because it might not be able to meet the needs of all stakeholder groups all the time. For example, some locals might not like heavy lorries trundling around at the weekend and during the night. However, if business survival depends on 24-hours-a-day operations, then it would have to ignore the locals or explain to them that stopping the lorries would lose jobs.

> ✎ This is a good conclusion that provides a well-judged and balanced view.

(2) Carnbridge Chemicals chose the safest processes rather than the most profitable ones. This is an example of ethical behaviour and making a morally correct decision. Ethical behaviour such as this may seem less profitable but in fact can be profitable both in the long run and in an indirect sense. If the public knows of such ethical decision-making, it can be a USP carrying marketing and competitive advantages. But I can't imagine why Carnbridge's customer would be really influenced by this because it doesn't sell its products to final consumers but to other firms. However, a lot of investors these days want to invest in ethical businesses, so that might benefit the company.

> ✎ Again, this answer begins with an explanation of key terms and then goes on to address the question by providing arguments supporting the view and relating these closely to Carnbridge Chemicals.

3

question

On the other hand, you could argue that such decisions actually reduce profits, especially if costs are higher and there is no effect on demand. But the case study says that a cost–benefit analysis was done taking account of external costs and benefits. So you could argue that profitability is when total financial and external or social benefits are greater than financial and external or social costs. Bill Leighton, the finance director, seems to think that this is the way to look at it and he has lots of experience in the chemical industry to back that up.

> This paragraph began with opposing arguments to those in the previous paragraph. It would have been useful to develop these further. However, the subsequent discussion of what might be meant by profit and its direct application to the case study is excellent.

(3) There might be a conflict between ethical decision-making and delegation. If managers who make delegated decisions have different ethical positions from those that the firm has and states in its mission statement, then they might not make decisions in line with the firm's ethics. That is where the conflict lies.

> This is a good response that simply but clearly states why conflict might arise between ethical decision-making and delegation.

On the basis of evidence in the case study, it doesn't seem as if there is this type of conflict at Carnbridge. All the people mentioned in the case study seem to be in tune with the firm and loyal to it. All their comments are positive about the firm and it's clear that the ethical decision about the new plant was unanimous. However, the fact that it took some time to check the situation suggests that delegation means there is not full awareness of actions being taken by sub-ordinates, and that an employee with different objectives might not be following company policy.

> As requested, the candidate has answered the question 'on the basis of the evidence'. Overall, this answer addresses both parts of the question posed in a relevant and knowledgeable way. However, the final part of the answer could have been clarified and extended further.

(4) Carnbridge Chemicals is facing some pressure group activity. It says the media is helping environmental pressure groups and that this could lead to a loss of business and goodwill. A pressure group is an organisation formed by people with a common interest who get together to further their interests.

> This defines pressure groups and sets the answer clearly within the context of the case study.

Pressure group activity in the case study is by direct action and encouraging the media interest in the leak. If the pressure groups can do this they can convince the public and thus increase their pressure on the company. This pressure group might be local, but with press coverage it could soon become national and get help from big and famous environmental pressure groups.

Such actions may cause a business to change its activity but will certainly change public opinion. But the case study suggests that the firm really is not responsible. In general, the success of a pressure group is determined by its financial resources, its reputation, the degree of public sympathy for its cause, and access to the media. The last two are probably most important in this situation.

 In analysing the possible impact on the firm of pressure group activity, the candidate clearly applies knowledge to the case study.

In order to minimise impact, the firm could consider either changing its activity or launching a PR campaign to counter the claims. In this case, the firm hasn't got anything to change if it's not guilty, so launching a PR campaign is the action the firm has chosen to minimise the impact of pressure groups. It seems the right thing to do in the circumstances.

 Good judgement is shown here, based on sound subject knowledge and an analysis of the situation.

(5) A social audit assesses the impact of a firm's activities on its stakeholders and on society. It includes details of a firm's activities in relation to pollution, waste, health and safety and consumers. The firm must identify its social objectives and its ethical values; it must define its stakeholders and measure its performance against specific performance indicators. The social accounts that provide this entire detail can then, like Carnbridge has done, be sent away to be independently audited, ready for publication. The benefits to organisations such as Carnbridge of social auditing are that it provides information to pressure groups and consumers and other stakeholders about the social responsibilities of business. It also identifies the extent to which a firm is meeting its non-financial objectives, employees gain a complete picture of the impact of their firm's activities, and it could deter future criticism, especially if, like Carnbridge, its social audit is independent.

 The answer provides convincing evidence of clear understanding of social auditing here. In addition, we have clear identification of the benefits to Carnbridge Chemicals. However, there is no analysis of these benefits and no evaluation either.

 The candidate's answers demonstrate clear subject knowledge, the ability to apply that knowledge to the case study and, most importantly, the ability to analyse issues and evaluate arguments. Unfortunately, in part 5, these higher-level skills are lacking, but the general level of answers overall would guarantee a good A grade.

■ ■ ■

Answer to question 3: candidate B

(1) Social responsibility makes good business sense. If you can get customers and workers and the local population to think well of you by treating them all well, then you'll make more sales and more money in the long term.

📝 There is no real explanation of what is meant by social responsibility in this answer other than 'treating them all well'. Some relevant points are made but in a somewhat cynical fashion that is not very convincing.

If you focus only on the responsibility to make profits for shareholders, you might demotivate workers, turn customers away and get a bad reputation with locals. So you'll make less profit in the long run.

📝 Again, some relevant issues are raised but it is not clear that the candidate really understands social responsibility or its implications.

(2) Carnbridge Chemicals didn't select the most profitable option because it wanted to make sure that the process it chose was safe. If it chose a less safe but more profitable process, this might not be the case in the long term because a leak would add to costs and reduce profits. So this type of ethical decision-making is probably more profitable in the long term. If it weren't, the firm probably wouldn't do it.

📝 Although the candidate suggests that long-term costs may be lower and profits higher, there is not an ethical dimension to the answer.

(3) Conflict can occur between ethical decision-making and delegation. It happens because of differences between the moral behaviour of people who make decisions on behalf of the firm and the moral position of a firm. It comes about because a firm consists of people who have their own moral principles and these could differ from the firm's culture and principles. If there is a lot of conflict here, then a firm like Carnbridge needs to do something about it. It could introduce training to ensure staff who are making decisions are in agreement with the firm.

📝 This discusses very clearly the potential conflict that can arise and how it might be dealt with. The only problem is that it does not consider this in relation to Carnbridge Chemicals as requested.

(4) Environmental pressure groups are putting pressure on the business and this could lead to fewer sales and bad publicity. Local media attention is increasing the pressure.

📝 The candidate indicates the possible impact on the firm, but the response is brief and rather superficial. More detailed analysis of the possible impact and some judgement are desirable given the request to assess.

It doesn't appear as if the company is responsible for the leak, so it seems a bit unfair. The company will have to show the public it wasn't responsible and it seems to be doing this by having a PR campaign with press releases and meetings and tours around the firm.

📝 This provides relevant information but it is descriptive, again lacking analysis and judgement as to whether this is the right course of action.

(5) A social audit tells you about how the firm's actions affect its stakeholders and everyone. It includes details on pollution, waste, health and safety and views of consumers. It means a firm must give its social objectives and ethical values, state who its stakeholders are, measure its performance against targets and, like Carnbridge, send these sorts of accounts off for independent audit and then publish the results. All of this is a good thing because it makes the firm look much better to the media and pressure groups that it will invite for a tour around.

This provides convincing evidence of the candidate's knowledge of social auditing but there is no consideration of the benefits to organisations in general or to Carnbridge Chemicals in particular.

The candidate has shown sound knowledge and understanding throughout the answers to this question. However, a major problem with these answers is the relative lack of analysis and the absence of evaluation based on such analysis. In addition, on a number of occasions, the question has not been fully addressed because there has been no reference back to the case study material. On this basis, the candidate would be awarded a **D** grade.

Impact on firms of a change in size

Haywood Ceramics

Haywood Ceramics had been in business for about 50 years. Based in Burslem in the Potteries area of the Midlands, it had grown from a small pottery to a large private limited company selling tableware worldwide. Jason Marlowe, the grandson of Haywood's founder, was its managing director. He had overseen significant growth in the business, including a new factory adjacent to the original one and a move into the US market.

Although the decision to grow had been successful at first, it had not been problem free and the board of this family-owned business had been divided on several issues:

- The first issue was whether to grow organically or via external means. The older family members wanted organic growth in order to maintain full control. The younger members, Jason included, had wanted to merge with another successful pottery firm that already had a footing in the international market. The older members won that battle. The decision still rankled with Jason, but the majority of shareholders had supported organic growth and — given that crucial decisions had always been taken on a vote — there was little he could do.
- Financing growth was another issue. Jason favoured floating the business in order to form a public limited company, but the older shareholders were insistent on keeping the business in the family. Once again, they won even though their decision narrowed the financial options available to the firm. However, financial control had always been excellent — if slightly conservative — and there were few problems in obtaining necessary finance.
- Establishing a market abroad was fairly straightforward as a result of the huge US demand for UK tableware. Because tastes and preferences for design and size were substantially different, Haywood Ceramics decided to separate the factory processes. Much of the work for the international market was in the original plant and the new plant specialised in domestic tableware.

Despite disagreements, Jason felt that the growth strategy had been successful. However, 3 years later the US market collapsed because the strength of the pound was making UK exports uncompetitive. At first Jason thought this might be a short-term problem, but it had persisted for almost 2 years to the point where substantial losses were being made and the old plant was operating at only 30% capacity.

The recent board meeting to discuss these problems was sombre. Some board members were in favour of closing the old plant, selling it off and concentrating on the domestic market. Jason felt this retrenchment to the position of 10 years ago was too radical and shortsighted and didn't take account of the fact that the external environment was constantly changing and that new opportunities might come along.

Then there was the possibility of a management buyout, an option suggested by some of the senior managers. Reactions of board members included:

'If we can't make it work, why do they think they can make a go of it?'

'It might safeguard jobs. Some of those workers have been with us for years.'

'But if they don't make a go of it, workers might actually be worse off.'

This whole debate was on the agenda of the next meeting when the management team interested in the buyout would provide more detailed proposals. In addition, other forms of retrenchment were to be considered, with the emphasis on protecting the workforce, many of whom had worked for Haywood for 20 years or more.

(1) Discuss the issues that are likely to have been considered by Haywood Ceramics in deciding how to finance its growth strategies. (14 marks)

(2) Haywood Ceramics is a private limited company but the text suggests that Jason is in favour of floating the company in order to form a plc. Assess the likely arguments that would have been involved in the decision to remain a private company. (14 marks)

(3) Consider what the 'other forms of retrenchment' to be discussed at the forthcoming board meeting are likely to be. Assess how these might affect the workforce and other stakeholder groups. (16 marks)

(4) Haywood Ceramics chose organic (or internal) growth. To what extent might external growth strategies have reduced the impact of the problems it subsequently encountered in the US market? (18 marks)

(5) Evaluate the possible risks and rewards to different stakeholder groups from a management buyout of the old plant. (18 marks)

Total: 80 marks

■ ■ ■

Answer to question 4: candidate A

(1) Growth had been organic or internal. The building or purchase of a new factory must have been expensive and it would also have cost a lot to establish the US sales operation. The important issues in deciding on the form of finance for any firm are about obtaining enough finance and getting the right type of finance.

✍ This is a reasonable introduction, identifying what the finance would be required for and indicating the important issues to consider.

As the company decided to remain a private limited company, a share issue would not be an appropriate form of finance. If it was looking to internal finance, retained profits, if sufficient, might have been useful for the factory. This is a traditional family firm, so the board may well choose this because it would probably take a long-term view of such developments. A factory would mean a fairly long-term form of finance, so external sources would probably involve a bank loan.

✍ This paragraph is succinct in discussing forms of finance relevant to the situation. It shows judgement and some analysis. Note how there has not been any time wasted describing the different sources of finance, but an immediate focus on the issues to be considered.

In general, the type of finance depends on a range of issues such as the type of legal structure of the business, which I've already mentioned. Haywood Ceramics is an established business, so it should have good collateral and a good reputation. It says financial control was excellent. The performance of the business and the economy was sound at the stage Haywood needed the finance to expand.

> Again, relevant issues are discussed here. It might have been better to include this paragraph earlier as it provides background analysis to support the judgement regarding the most relevant forms of finance for this situation.

(2) Remaining a private limited company means being able to maintain more privacy and flexibility than a public limited company. As a plc, a business has to make public how it is performing, and the press and other groups are constantly scrutinising performance. This puts more pressure on management that must also keep an eye on daily share price movements. It encourages a focus on short- rather than long-term issues.

> This is a good paragraph that considers the important issues involved in any decision about the legal status of a company. It shows clear understanding and analysis.

Staying a private limited company means the original family can maintain control more easily, there are none or very few of the problems of divorce and ownership as you get in large plc organisations, and the company still has the most important thing — limited liability. On the other hand, there are less sources of finance available, but whether this is a problem or not depends on the company. I don't think it was an issue with Haywood Ceramics. But I think they would have disliked the problems I mentioned above associated with plc status so would prefer to stay a private limited company.

> Sound analysis of issues is provided and some judgement is shown in relation to Haywood Ceramics. However, the last sentence lacks substance; it needs supporting with more detail on why they 'would prefer to stay a private limited company'.

(3) The board's previous discussion had been about closing the old plant, so 'other forms of retrenchment' includes things such as stopping recruitment, early retirement and voluntary redundancy. This would probably reduce job insecurity but the company may lose key staff. Another thing it could do is rationalise the business by delayering. This means less impact on the shop floor but a greater workload for remaining managers and fewer promotion prospects as jobs disappear. Another option is making targeted cutbacks and redundancies throughout the firm. This means the business can still meet its objectives. It also means it could get rid of problem staff or staff who aren't productive. But it will make people feel insecure and worry whether it will be them next.

🖉 This is a solid paragraph demonstrating sound knowledge and clear analysis of implications for the workforce. The question does, however, ask for a consideration of 'other stakeholder groups' as well, which is not provided.

Given that a management buyout is possible, delayering might be the best option since a whole group of managers is likely to go anyway and this might allow some reorganisation and perhaps other jobs could be enriched or enlarged.

🖉 A conclusion that shows sensible judgement based on the events in the text.

(4) Organic or internal growth means growing larger by expanding the existing business. External growth means merging or taking over another firm. This type of growth can include backward or forward vertical integration, where a company like Haywood might integrate with a supplier of clay or retailer of the pots. It could include horizontal integration, where a company might merge with a competitor. It could also include conglomerate integration — joining with a firm that is in an unrelated line of business.

🖉 A good, if lengthy, introduction that demonstrates the candidate's clear understanding of the various external growth strategies available.

The question asks whether either of these types of external growth would have lessened the drop in US sales. Vertical integration backwards wouldn't really make any difference, but if Haywood had merged forward with a retailer in America, this might have made a difference because sales would then be in dollars. Horizontal would probably not have made a difference unless it was with a US pottery firm. Another UK pottery firm, even with a footing in the international market, would still have been hit by the strength of the pound. Conglomerate is more difficult to assess because it depends on the products involved and where they are sold.

🖉 This paragraph contains some relevant analysis and judgement but the argument related to each strategy is rather brief.

Basically, anything that means selling abroad would require exchange rate transactions and face the same problems. Only those strategies that can avoid such transactions would have avoided this.

🖉 The candidate draws a reasonable conclusion based on the previous analysis.

(5) A management buyout is where managers buy a part of the company they run. I suppose they hope to be able to make the older factory and/or the US market profitable.

🖉 Defining terms, as here, is always a useful starting-point for an answer.

The rewards include a more motivated workforce and management team, perhaps because the management is personally responsible and workers know this is a sort of second chance for them. There could be less conflict with the traditional family owners out of the way and a management buyout team of senior managers newly installed. For the same reason, objectives might be much clearer and the whole thing about bureaucracy and decision-making might change.

However, the risks to the management buyout team are great because if it fails they are likely to suffer personal losses. A major risk is that mentioned in the case study; if Haywood Ceramics can't make a go of it, why should the buyout team be able to? Even though some jobs might be saved, such actions usually involve rationalisation and job losses in order to improve the financial position, thus affecting morale.

 On the basis of the information in the case study and the candidate's subject knowledge, this analysis of risks and rewards is persuasive and relevant, focusing on two stakeholder groups, workers and managers.

If, however, it is successful, what often happens is that management might float the company or sell shares in a takeover. Both of these can give them massive reward, but what about the workers?

 In a question such as this, it is good to see an introduction, a substantial and well-argued paragraph on each aspect and then a conclusion. This is a controversial but not inappropriate conclusion, although more detail on the implications for workers would have been more valuable than ending with a question.

 Overall, these are good answers that demonstrate clear knowledge and application to the scenario provided. They provide detailed analysis on most of the issues raised and evaluation is in general well judged. This answer would achieve an A grade.

■ ■ ■

Answer to question 4: candidate B

(1) The types of finance available are numerous. Internal sources include retained profit, controlling working capital, sale and leaseback of assets. External sources include short-term ones such as trade credit, debt factoring and overdraft. Long-term sources include share capital and bank loan.

 This is simply a list of sources of finance, with no reference to the question.

Any company has to have funding that fits its needs. This is a private limited company so it isn't going to offer shares to the public, but it could get a bank loan. It mainly wants finance to build a factory, so it has to be this or retained profit because it is longer term.

 Relevant issues are raised here, but none is developed sufficiently.

(2) The advantages of a private limited company include limited liability and more capital than a sole trader or partnership but less than a plc. There is more privacy and flexibility than a plc and fewer legal formalities but fewer options for finance.

> 🖉 These statements are all correct and are related to legal status, but they are not addressing the question posed.

They probably decided to stay as a private limited company because they didn't want the endless examination of everything they do, like Marks and Spencer. Richard Branson from Virgin and Anita Roddick from the Body Shop went back from being a plc to private limited company for this reason.

> 🖉 This is a relevant and well-judged conclusion. It is just a pity that there was no previous analysis to support it.

(3) Retrenchment means cutting back in size. Shutting down a plant has many effects: it reduces fixed costs and other costs. It can lead to better capacity utilisation in other areas, though not in this case because the two factories specialise.

> 🖉 These statements are correct but the question asked about 'other forms of retrenchment', i.e. other than shutting the plant.

One of the problems is what Jason thought. There is no going back on this and once the factory has gone, it has gone. Lots of staff with really excellent skills will be lost. They could try something else like offering early retirement, voluntary redundancy or stop recruiting new people. Doing this would make people feel more secure and still cut down staff, without having to get rid of the factory.

> 🖉 The candidate has not read the question properly. The last sentence is the basis of a relevant answer but is provided as an afterthought.

(4) External growth involves integrating with other firms. It can take three different forms. Firstly, vertical — this can mean backward vertical where you merge with suppliers, therefore controlling quality, or forward vertical which controls the marketing of products to consumers. Both types mean you take all of the profit. Secondly, horizontal — this is between similar firms and leads to economies of scale, reduced competition and higher market share. Thirdly, conglomerate — this is merging with a firm in a completely different area and brings diversification and reduced risk.

> 🖉 The candidate is demonstrating clear knowledge and understanding of this area of the specification but is not relating it to the question.

None of this is anything to do with the strength of the pound, so these other growth strategies wouldn't reduce problems.

> 🖉 The candidate has not thought this conclusion through at all, and it would gain no credit.

(5) A management buyout is when an existing management team buys or takes over a part or all of a business. In this case, the management might want to use a different approach to the present owners.

> 🖉 This is a good introduction that defines the key term.

The risks and rewards depend on who you are. Management might risk losing their investment but otherwise they could end up mega-rich. If the buyout is successful and the business prospers, the owners could probably float it or sell their shares in a takeover. For the workers, it's all uncertain. A buyout may protect jobs but it could lead to worse job losses later.

Although brief, this paragraph is highly relevant. It contains some analysis and judgement but needs developing further in order to consider and assess the risks and rewards more thoroughly.

The candidate demonstrates confident knowledge and understanding of the subject. Some analysis and evaluation are provided but generally this is either weak or brief. In addition, answers often fail to address questions appropriately and would lose marks. As a consequence, this response would achieve an E grade.

Business objectives

Oxygene and UBT

All in all, Maddy Paxman thinks her move from Oxygene has been a good one. It was certainly a relief to join UBT Holdings plc and she was pleased when UBT promoted her within a year.

Oxygene is a private limited company run by Max Brown, a creative entrepreneur who is its major shareholder. His company is principally a design consultancy, but has offshoots in fashion, advertising and cosmetics. It is high profile, mainly because of Max Brown's charm and his popularity with the media. On leaving university, Maddy was thrilled to be working for a successful business with a mission and a culture that emphasised quality, style and informality.

She loved Oxygene at first. Everyone worked late almost every night, went to a bar or club after work and socialised at weekends. However, it was intensely competitive. Her colleagues were constantly trying to better one another, whether in securing deals, arriving early, or working late. What had initially seemed hectic and exciting to Maddy appeared less enjoyable when experience taught her that everything was geared around Max. If he had a new idea, then it was picked up by everyone and became the most important thing. The competitiveness tended to be about pleasing Max, responding to his whims or looking good by achieving the targets he set. Much of this was related to the fact that potentially high salaries were determined on an individual basis with Max.

Maddy recognised Max's talents and thought that when Oxygene was new and small, Max had probably been an effective owner/boss. She didn't think he had adapted to running a large company and felt that he wasn't really able to delegate. Her view was that Max's inability to let go was influencing staff behaviour. In addition, she found her cautious nature was at odds with an ethos that was all about taking risks if there was a chance of success. Sometimes she'd felt that a more risk-averse approach might have been a better approach.

Maddy found the set-up too stressful, competitive, risky and dominated by Max's personality, and was relieved when a design assistant's job came up at UBT Holdings plc. UBT is a long-established corporation that employs thousands of people and has thorough recruitment procedures. There were many applicants on the short list for Maddy's job and she went through a series of tests and interviews. It was utterly different to the selection process at Oxygene, where, basically, if Max liked your work and liked you, the job was yours.

At UBT, Maddy has a detailed job description, fixed hours and holidays and there is a clear hierarchical structure. Maddy quickly learned the job, understood the organisation and even recognised its shortcomings. For example, there are many procedures that must be followed to the letter. She learned that when you ask someone to do something that isn't precisely within their job description, they often respond by saying it isn't their responsibility. Decision-making is slow, people sometimes fail to use their initiative and risks are rarely taken.

5

question

On the positive side, Maddy has targets to meet that she recognises as contributing to the overall corporate objectives. She feels committed to achieving these targets and to the corporation's mission statement and its emphasis on customer service, employee satisfaction and responsibility to the community. Her colleagues are also committed to UBT's general aims and this is the thing she likes most. Back at Oxygene, everyone was committed to pleasing Max Brown in the hope of improving their salaries. Looking back, she had never really felt the Oxygene mission statements were anything other than a public relations exercise.

(1) In relation to Oxygene and UBT Holdings plc, discuss the value of a mission statement and how mission statements are linked to organisational culture.   (14 marks)

(2) Assess the type of organisational culture that seems evident in UBT Holdings plc and how this might influence its decision-making.   (14 marks)

(3) To what extent does the organisational culture evident in Oxygene influence the behaviour of employees and how might you go about changing this culture?   (16 marks)

(4) As Oxygene has grown, Max Brown's role has changed from that of owner/boss to owner/manager. Discuss the problems that such a change in role might cause for an organisation.   (18 marks)

(5) A number of stakeholder groups are mentioned in the text. Consider the extent to which the aims of these various groups are in common with, or conflict with, the corporate aims and mission statements of the relevant organisation.   (18 marks)

Total: 80 marks

■ ▩ ■

Answer to question 5: candidate A

(1) A mission statement basically states the reason for an organisation's existence. It tells all the stakeholders what the firm is in business for and provides a justification for employees in terms of what the company stands for. For example, a mission statement spells out corporate concerns about the environment, or customers and employees, or quality and technology issues. The employees should know from the mission statement where the company intends to go and how it stands on certain issues.

🖉 This is a comprehensive, if rather lengthy, explanation of the term 'mission statement'.

The culture of an organisation affects the mission and aims and objectives of the company and also its decision-making procedures and behaviour. In this sense, a mission statement can shape the culture of a company. But you could argue that the common beliefs and values of employees should be the same as the values in a mission statement. It's a bit of a chicken and egg situation.

🖉 This is a rather complex response, but it does illustrate clearly the relationship between mission and culture.

Maddy says Oxygene's mission statement is really just a PR exercise, something that is produced to look good or because it seems the right thing to do. Its mission and culture are about style, quality and informality. But then Maddy says people were basically out for themselves. UBT's mission is about customer service, employee satisfaction and responsibility to the community. She says that all the people she worked with there seemed really committed to this, so here the mission seems really important in influencing culture. I suppose you could say that this is also true for Oxygene, it's just that its mission doesn't appear to be about the usual issues. It is more personal, and strongly influenced by Max Brown.

🖉 Here the candidate is applying knowledge to the two companies in the case study. Although some judgement is shown, there is little analysis — only a repetition of detail in the text.

(2) There are different types of organisational cultures. Two important ones are bureaucratic and entrepreneurial cultures. UBT has a bureaucratic culture. This is because the emphasis is on the roles people play rather than the individuals who play them. Maddy mentioned her detailed job description and the clear hier-archical structure. Also, UBT is not into the kind of risk-taking that made Maddy stressed at Oxygene. One of the features of bureaucratic cultures is that they are not very dynamic. Maddy suggests that this is the case because people don't often use their initiative and decision-making is slow with lots of procedures to go through.

🖉 An appropriate culture has been identified for UBT and some of the characteris-tics of such a culture are analysed in relation to the company.

Lots of the points about a bureaucratic culture seem to be negative, but they don't need to be because this type of organisation is likely to be able to survive and adapt gradually to the changes around it. Just like big government departments, big corporations are very similar and people tend to make careers in them for life.

🖉 A conclusion or evaluation here could have been about whether one culture or another was appropriate. This judgement is, however, no less valid, and demon-strates the positive and negative sides of the particular culture identified.

(3) Oxygene's organisational culture is more of an entrepreneurial culture, with emphasis on results and using initiative. There is lots of risk-taking, which can lead to success but might lead to failure, and it's very much about projects and tasks, with people being flexible about what they do. There is less of a hierarchy and it's all about results. This sort of power culture has a strong influence on the behaviour of employees who are competitive, committed to getting deals and meeting targets, even if that is not always the best thing to do.

🖉 This paragraph identifies a relevant culture for the organisation and impresses by using another and similar classification — power culture — to explain this further. Appropriate characteristics are analysed in the context of Oxygene.

To change the culture means starting at the top and changing the way the owner behaves, since it seems that he is driving this culture. The mission statement and aims and objectives need to be reviewed and the roles people have within the firm — especially in relation to the owner — need to alter before any changes in behaviour are likely to take place.

☑ Given what is known of this company from the text, this is a well-judged response.

(4) Max Brown is the owner of the business. Maddy says that he was probably a very effective owner/boss but not able to delegate or let go as the business has grown. This is not uncommon when someone sets up a small business that becomes successful. Growth is always difficult to manage and management needs to think this through carefully.

☑ This uses the information in the text to introduce the issue of growth and the owner/boss/manager relationship clearly.

As it grows, its structure changes and the hierarchy becomes more complex and different levels of authority will be needed to make decision-making effective. Perhaps this is not happening or has not been really thought through at Oxygene. Also, more delegation is needed as a business grows. If the original owner doesn't let go and accept that he will have less contact and should be taking more of a coordinator role, the problems will occur again. The other important point is to be able to manage and motivate the team. On one level Max is doing this, but it's more about getting them to compete than getting them all to feel OK with the set up.

☑ The candidate demonstrates sound knowledge and the ability to analyse the issues in the context of Oxygene.

Despite all these issues, we are only told the story from Maddy's point of view. It might be that all is working well. There is nothing that says the company is unsuccessful or that lots of staff are leaving.

☑ Although not the conclusion one might expect, this does demonstrate judgement in the context of the information and is therefore valid.

(5) For Oxygene, the stakeholder groups mentioned include the owner and workers. For the owner, the objectives are his personal ones but the situation with the workers is a bit more difficult. Maddy's aims are in conflict with the mission and aims of Oxygene, which is why she decided to leave. So if the other workers are like her, this will be the same. But the other employees seem quite committed to the mission and aims. They wouldn't work so hard or be so competitive, unless they are intimidated or insecure. This seems to be what Maddy thinks.

☑ This is a convincing response demonstrating analysis and evaluation, and based firmly on information in the text.

For UBT, its mission and aims seem to be in common with the stakeholder groups mentioned — mainly employees but also customers and community. If the aims of stakeholder groups conflict with those of the company, this causes problems.

Basically, a company can't satisfy all groups all the time and has to try to prioritise and compromise.

🖉 The reference to UBT is superficial and needs further consideration. The final two sentences are perfectly valid in a conclusion but need developing to demonstrate — in the context of the previous analysis — the implications of prioritising and compromising.

🖉 **The candidate has produced answers that demonstrate sound knowledge and understanding and an ability to apply that knowledge to the context of the case study. The candidate has used the information provided in the text admirably in producing answers that are in general analytical and evaluative. On this basis, an A grade would be awarded.**

■ ■ ■

Answer to question 5: candidate B

(1) Mission statements tell you what a company thinks is important in terms of broad aims such as customer care and green issues. Organisational culture is the way people behave in a firm and their values and beliefs. The mission influences the culture because the priorities set down in the mission are what everyone should be trying to achieve. However, the culture will influence the mission because the culture reflects the behaviour of people who set up the mission.

🖉 The key terms are explained in a paragraph that – albeit briefly — also demonstrates the link between mission and culture. There is, however, no discussion about the value of the mission statement.

Oxygene and UBT have different mission statements and cultures because they are different types of organisations in terms of size, legal structure, history and leadership style.

🖉 This sentence contains issues that could be explored. As it is, they are only identified.

(2) UBT's organisational culture is a role one. This is the type of culture found in big bureaucracies governed by rules and procedures rather than values of particular individuals. Role cultures tend to have slow decision-making and lack of initiative in contrast to a power culture like Oxygene.

🖉 The candidate identifies an appropriate culture to describe UBT and provides some explanation, but the answer does not contain analysis or evaluation.

(3) Oxygene has a power culture that is influenced by its owner Max Brown. A successful entrepreneur, Max likes people to take risks and use their initiative. He determines how the organisation operates. The point here is whether or not Max wants the culture changed. If he doesn't, nothing will happen. Should the company become unsuccessful, then Max might want to look at its aims and objectives, its mission and what it stands for. Changes in these and in Max's attitude could influence and change the culture.

🖉 Again, an appropriate culture is identified and explained using detail from the text. There is some judgement shown that is valid but it needs developing and under-pinning with more detailed analysis.

(4) Max Brown doesn't seem to have too many problems looking after his business and it seems very successful. However, changing from owner/boss to owner/manager can cause problems. As a manager you have to motivate staff, so you have to have the right style and not be too autocratic. You have to be able to give a bit of control to other people because you can't do everything yourself. Max Brown wasn't able to delegate or let go, so this is a problem he is having.

🖉 The first sentence adds little and is not linked to the rest of the paragraph. However, the rest is good. Appropriate issues are raised and analysed in terms of the case study context.

These are mainly people problems, so basically you've got to make sure you can manage people and not just the business itself. Making a product or providing a service is only part of the problem.

🖉 There is some evaluation in this concluding paragraph and it is based on the preceding discussion.

(5) A company has many different stakeholders. They include workers, customers, shareholders and basically any group with an interest in the company.

🖉 This is a good start that explains the concept.

Companies need to try to keep all these groups satisfied. If not, they might lose custom, investors and staff. If the mission and aims of a company are acceptable to the stakeholders, everything should be OK. If they aren't, then there are problems.

🖉 This is a weak response. What it says is accurate but it includes no analysis of the points made and includes no evaluation.

🖉 **Knowledge and understanding of the subject are generally convincing in these answers. There is some analysis and evaluation, for example in questions 3 and 4, but in general evidence of these higher-level skills is weak. This response would achieve a D/E grade.**

Business strategy

SehrSchön

At 10 a.m. the board members were assembled and Patrick Wexford was nervous. As a final-year business management undergraduate on placement at SehrSchön, his dissertation project was to come up with strategic options for the company's directors. His presentation was to be the third item on the agenda.

SehrSchön makes high-quality chocolate bars and a small range of beautifully packaged chocolate selections. The products are handmade, expensive and aimed at exclusive chocolate markets in the UK and western Europe and to a lesser extent North America. Given the reputation for chocolate production in France, Belgium, Germany and Switzerland, Patrick could understand the pride the directors take in having broken into these markets.

SehrSchön is a small private limited company located on an old and established industrial estate, where there are always units available for sale or rent. The company is reasonably successful and profits have been fairly constant, in real terms, for the last few years. There are competitors but, at this end of the market, not that many of them. Customers tend to be long-standing and gained by personal contact and word of mouth.

As part of his research, Patrick had completed an internal and external analysis of the company. He found it to be a well-managed and financially sound company. However, he had noted a slight downward trend in profits, which matched a similar slight downward trend in sales. He knew that the nature of SehrSchön's products and its target market made it difficult to cut costs further — handmade chocolates had to be handmade, that's what allowed SehrSchön the huge premium on price.

Patrick had identified six serious competitors, all based in western Europe. They had similar market shares, although he had heard that a company in Belgium had been stepping up its promotion activities and had managed to increase its market share. Given the legal status of these companies — each one a private limited company — it was difficult to get any clear evidence of this. He had also heard that a Swiss producer was having difficulties and was considering selling up or closing down. It had made an apparently unsuccessful attempt to diversify into the sugar confectionery market (sweets, toffees and gums). Patrick had seen the advertising and thought it tacky and poorly targeted. He felt that with a bit of thought and an emphasis on words like 'quality', 'old fashioned', 'traditional' and 'handmade', sugar confectionery could be targeted at the same market as the exclusive chocolates.

Patrick noted that despite recession, rising unemployment and falling rates of economic growth, sales of chocolate at this end of the market had been more or less unaffected. Neither had export sales been hit much by the strength of the pound. He concluded that the products were both price and income inelastic. Internationally, the mass chocolate and sugar confectionery market was dominated by companies like CadburySchweppes and Mars. They had been busy in eastern Europe, in countries like Poland, but didn't touch the exclusive end of those markets.

The first item on the agenda was about the company's long-term aims. The consensus was that SehrSchön was a traditional family company and this is what it intended to stay. The aims were to do with quality, tradition and craftsmanship. As far as Patrick could see, this emphasis influenced everything and everyone in the organisation from the ladies in the canteen to the managing director. It was probably a reason why the company had been around so long, had managed to get into western European markets, and had been awarded a royal seal of approval.

The second agenda item was about a problem that had occurred 6 months earlier when faulty storage conditions had damaged a batch of chocolates in the USA. The buyer, a chain of exclusive shops, had cancelled all future orders and a large portion of US sales were lost. Having visited the USA and discovered that a warehouse contractor was to blame, the marketing director had managed to get the order back, but the whole episode had made SehrSchön vulnerable. Patrick wondered why the company hadn't dealt with this problem earlier. Faulty storage is not an entirely unpredictable difficulty; contingency plans should have been in place.

'Next on the agenda is item 3. Over to you Patrick.'

Patrick walked to the overhead projector he had requested. He had decided to consider the strategic options open to the company using Ansoff's matrix and then to look in detail at one of the options he was considering — the possibility of introducing a new product to the existing market — using a decision tree approach (see Box 1).

OPTION 1	**Introducing a new product**
Costs	Introducing new product = £600,000
Probabilities	Introduce new product; competitor introduces new product = 0.8
	Introduce new product; competitor does not introduce new product = 0.2
Pay-offs	+£750,000, if competitor introduces new product
	+£1,250,000, if competitor does not introduce new product
OPTION 2	**Do nothing**
Costs	Do nothing = £0
Probabilities	Do nothing; competitor introduces new product = 0.4
	Do nothing; competitor does not introduce new product = 0.6
Pay-offs	−£500,000 if the competitor introduces new product
	+£500,000 if the competitor does not introduce new product

Box 1   Introducing a new product — decision tree information

Patrick finished as planned at 1 p.m. Everyone had looked interested and he really had managed to grab their attention. This really would make a fantastic dissertation — he might even get a first with it.

(1) **To what extent do external factors influence the success of a company such as SehrSchön?**

(14 marks)

(2) **With reference to SehrSchön, discuss the extent to which the mission statement and objectives of the company influence its organisational culture and potential success.**

(14 marks)

(3) **Using Ansoff's matrix, assess the strategic options available to SehrSchön.** (16 marks)

(4) (a) **Using the information provided, construct a decision tree and calculate the expected value of each option.**

(6 marks)

   (b) **Is the decision tree analysis in (4)(a) sufficient for effective decision-making? Justify your answer.**

(12 marks)

(5) **Patrick felt that contingency planning should be in place at SehrSchön. Evaluate how this might contribute to the success of the operations of a company such as SehrSchön.**

(18 marks)

Total: 80 marks

■ ■ ■

Answer to question 6: candidate A

(1) External factors influence any company. They can be opportunities or threats and are often not under the company's control.

☑ An introduction sets the scene for the rest of the answer. It would have been useful to indicate what is meant by external influences.

The external economic factors mentioned include recession, rising unemployment, falling economic growth and a strong pound. Generally, these would be real threats to a company selling at home and abroad, but this doesn't seem to be the case with SehrSchön. This is because the chocolates are aimed at the premium end of the market and are price and income inelastic. So, if prices rise or average incomes fall, sales won't be affected. The customers are probably so wealthy that any price rise won't have any effect and their incomes would have to fall a lot to damage sales. For products that are not inelastic, these economic factors would have a bad effect. The mass-market products sold by Cadbury's and Mars would probably be price and income elastic and so would be more affected than SehrSchön's products.

☑ This is sound analysis that is detailed and relevant and is applied directly to the context.

Other external factors could include the level of competition and what competitors are doing. A small firm in a massive market with lots of other small firms is probably quite safe. But although SehrSchön is small, it is only in a small market

6
question

with six serious competitors and so any change in one of its competitors will have effects on the others. One of its competitors seems to be expanding and one closing down, meaning there might be opportunities and threats.

✍ The candidate gives another relevant strand in the discussion of external influences.

Other external factors include government and social effects, but these aren't mentioned in the text and are unlikely to be relevant. Because this market is traditional, small and exclusive, it seems to be protected from external influences.

✍ This is a well-judged conclusion, based on the foregoing analysis.

(2) A mission statement gives the basic aims and purpose of the business. The culture of a company is the system of beliefs and values held by the firm and people in it. This is usually influenced by the mission statement, which in turn reflects the culture.

✍ This is a good introduction that explains the key terms and the relationship between them.

The case study says this is a traditional family company and not a plc. The company's aims and mission are about quality, tradition and craftsmanship and it has the royal seal for its products. It has been around for a long time and this seems to influence the culture because all employees are in tune with it from the canteen ladies to the MD. This is probably why SehrSchön is so well established. The fact that it is a private, limited, traditional family company probably supports this culture. For this particular company, its mission and culture seem exactly right for the market it is in. The staff are motivated and committed to provide exclusive, handmade and high-quality products.

✍ This response addresses the question directly using information from the text and the candidate's subject knowledge to determine how much mission affects culture and in turn success.

(3) Ansoff's matrix has four boxes for four different strategic options.

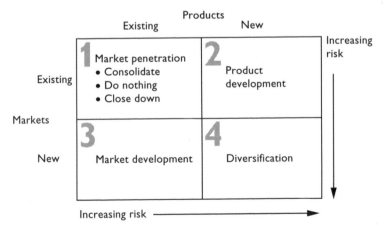

☑ The diagram is correct and complete.

(1) Existing products/existing markets such as doing nothing or penetrating the market even further.

(2) New product/existing markets such as developing or modifying or changing products for the same customers.

(3) Existing products/new markets such as selling to new geographic areas.

(4) New products/new markets such as diversifying completely.

These different options have different levels of risk. Diversification is the most risky, whereas just trying to increase market share is less risky.

☑ The candidate has demonstrated clear understanding of Ansoff's matrix. However, explaining it in detail like this and then applying it to the question is a rather lengthy approach and would not gain additional marks.

SehrSchön could try to increase market share in its present markets by trying to pick up sales from the Swiss producer that seems to be in difficulty and stop sales going to the Belgian firm. This would require an increase in marketing efforts, a low-risk option that would, however, require more money.

SehrSchön could try what the Swiss company has failed to do, and make high-quality sweets as well as chocolate. Patrick seems to think this might be something that could be achieved. However, it is more risky selling new products to existing markets.

It could try to sell its existing products in other countries. Since it has got such a good reputation, this might be worth trying.

Finally, it could try producing sweets and selling them in a new market, either in other countries or to a lower end of the market.

☑ This section takes each of the strategic options in Ansoff's matrix and considers how they could be applied to SehrSchön. It demonstrates good analysis and some evaluation.

Before deciding, the company needs to consider the risks and what it really wants to do given its history and mission. The lower end of the market is probably not appropriate. Its sales and profits are falling slightly, so it needs to do something. Opportunities in Europe or the USA either to penetrate the market or to sell to new markets in other countries would probably be cheaper to implement. Going into sweets would require a whole new process and lots of investment and it is not clear that SehrSchön actually wants to expand. In addition, going into sweets is likely to reduce its exclusive image.

☑ This is a thoughtful and appropriate conclusion that demonstrates excellent skills of analysis and evaluation throughout.

question

(4) (a)

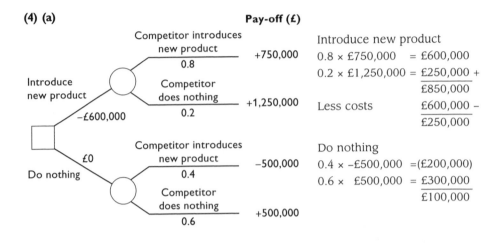

Pay-off (£)

Competitor introduces new product — 0.8 — +750,000

Introduce new product — −£600,000

Competitor does nothing — 0.2 — +1,250,000

£0

Do nothing

Competitor introduces new product — 0.4 — −500,000

Competitor does nothing — 0.6 — +500,000

Introduce new product
0.8 × £750,000 = £600,000
0.2 × £1,250,000 = £250,000 +
£850,000
Less costs £600,000 −
£250,000

Do nothing
0.4 × −£500,000 = (£200,000)
0.6 × £500,000 = £300,000
£100,000

 This is a correct analysis using the decision tree approach; all the calculations are correct and the working is clear.

(4) (b) Decision tree analysis encourages a careful consideration of all the alternatives and helps to set out the problems clearly and logically. It means that quantitative data are used rather then just someone's view. The probability means that risks of failure are being taken into account.

 Candidate A makes a clear statement of the benefits of decision tree analysis, which needs to be balanced with the possible problems before drawing conclusions about its value.

However, this is quite a major decision and it involves a lot more thought than just a few figures. It means expansion and perhaps a totally new outlook for the firm, and possibly new skills and new contacts. These figures are Patrick's and he hasn't said where they came from or how he got them. Has he done enough market research? The text mentions that evidence is hard to come by because the competitors are all private limited companies. Also the calculation in (4)(a) suggests that SehrSchön ought to go ahead but the return is only £150,000 more than doing nothing, so is it really worth it? On the other hand, will this move lead to other developments later? It depends on the objectives of the company, but the information from the decision tree analysis is not enough to make such an important decision.

 This is an excellent paragraph. It combines a discussion of the problems of using decision trees with a soundly argued judgement as to why it would be inappropriate to base decision-making on this information alone in this case.

(5) Contingency planning is planning to deal with predictable and quantifiable crises or unexpected and unwelcome events. It usually means that a firm has recognised a crisis might occur. It has thought of all the different situations that might happen and done 'what if' exercises — often by computer. It will have tried to find ways to prevent each crisis and made plans for dealing with them if they occur.

e This is a good paragraph that explains what contingency planning is and what is involved.

In SehrSchön's case, the problem was something that it should have thought about before. Patrick thought it was a fairly predictable type of problem. Knowing this, it should have recognised that its image would be threatened. The marketing director did a good PR job in getting the customer back, but perhaps the company should really have had extra checks in place and ways of dealing with the problem immediately rather than 6 months after the event.

e The idea of contingency planning is related directly to the situation in the case. There is some analysis and some evaluation evident.

e **This is a clear A-grade script in which the candidate focuses on the questions and uses information from the text. Convincing judgement based on sound analysis together with clear knowledge and understanding of theory and concepts are demonstrated throughout.**

■ ■ ■

Answer to question 6: candidate B

(1) SehrSchön sells to countries in Europe, so it might be affected by the UK's decision not to join the euro. It says its sales are not affected by the strong pound because they are price inelastic — in other words, if prices go up abroad because of the pound, this won't stop people buying. Similarly, recession, rising unemployment and falling economic growth will all mean incomes fall — but since the chocolates are income inelastic, this won't affect them.

e This paragraph contains relevant issues and some analysis.

This company is lucky because it sells in a high-class market and so isn't affected by things that affect ordinary markets.

e Although the candidate could have given further explanation, this is a reasonably well-judged conclusion that stems from the previous analysis.

(2) A mission statement and objectives influence organisational culture. A mission statement states the purpose of a business, and the culture is the principal values of the staff of the company. If these fit together well, they should allow the company to perform well. This also means that workers understand what the company is about and work towards achieving its goals so that it can be successful.

e The content of this paragraph is accurate and provides a sound basis for the rest of the answer. Unfortunately, nothing else is provided even though the question states 'with reference to SehrSchön'.

(3)

Products

Existing | New

	Existing		New
Existing	Market penetration		Product development
Markets			
New	Market development		Diversification

✎ The diagram is accurate and more or less complete, although the degree of risk needs to be added.

SehrSchön could choose any of these options. What it chooses will depend on its objectives — whether it wants to diversify; the money it has available; whether it wants to invest in new plant; and also what its competitors are doing.

✎ This is too brief and demonstrates no analysis of the options that SehrSchön could select. However, it does raise relevant issues for consideration and shows some judgement.

(4) (a)

	Competitors do 0.8	750,000	Introduce new product
Introduce			$0.8 \times £750,000 = £600,000$
	Competitors don't 0.2	1,250,000	$0.2 \times £1,250,000 = £250,000 +$
			£850,000
	Competitors do 0.4	500,000	Do nothing
Do nothing			$0.4 \times £500,000 = £200,000$
	Competitors don't 0.6	500,000	$0.6 \times £500,000 = £300,000 +$
			£500,000

✎ The candidate has forgotten to deduct the costs of introducing a new product and has not recognised that doing nothing when competitors introduce a new product actually incurs a negative sum and not a positive one. However, 'own figure rules' would apply, allowing the answer to pick up marks for the correct aspects of the answer and the generally correct process.

(4) (b) The decision tree analysis in (4)(a) shows clearly that introducing a new product is much better than doing nothing. This sort of analysis gives a numerate and logical approach to problem-solving that is better than a gut reaction.

✎ This response provides only one side of the answer. No consideration is given to the problems of using decision tree analysis either generally or in context.

(5) If a firm is prepared for a crisis, it is able to deal with it more easily. If the crisis is fairly predictable and can be prepared for in advance, this is contingency planning. SehrSchön's problem was a fairly normal one for a chocolate maker and so it should have had plans in place to deal with it immediately. It nearly lost a major customer. I suppose now this has happened once, it will do something about it and be prepared to cope if it happens again.

🖉 This answer demonstrates some understanding of contingency planning generally and in relation to the case study. Some judgement is shown based on supporting argument, but this could have been developed and extended.

🖉 **This candidate demonstrates understanding of concepts and theory in each of these answers and, generally, the issues raised are relevant. However, analysis and evaluation tend to be absent or brief and are sometimes unrelated to the context as requested by the question. On this basis, the candidate would have achieved a borderline C grade.**